The Growplan Vegetable Book

A Month-by-Month Guide

Written and edited by
Peter Peskett and Geoff Amos

With contributions from
Beryl Cutforth, Ray Edwards,
Geoff Hamilton and Les Jones

David & Charles
Newton Abbot London North Pomfret (Vt) Vancouver

ISBN 0 7153 7621 7

Printed in Great Britain by A. Wheaton and Co Ltd, Exeter
for David & Charles (Publishers) Limited
Brunel House Newton Abbot Devon

Published in the United States of America
by David & Charles Inc
North Pomfret Vermont 05053 USA

Published in Canada
by Douglas David & Charles Limited
1875 Welch Street North Vancouver BC

Contents

Introduction

Ten years ago, a friend of mine ripped up his large vegetable plot, carefully levelled the ground and sowed a superb 'billiard-table' lawn in its place. I was flabbergasted. He was a good vegetable grower and his immaculate produce was the envy of the neighbours.

'Why?' I asked him as I stood in a state of shock, looking at what had once been one of the most productive vegetable patches I'd seen. Now it was peppered with stumpy stems of grass knitting themselves into a lawn. 'What on earth did you do that for?'

'Vegetables are such a time-consuming job,' my friend said. 'I've enjoyed growing them, but I only did it because I had to.' While his three children were still living at home, a garden full of fresh produce virtually all-year-round had helped him eke out the family budget. 'There's no doubt we saved a lot of money by growing our own. But with the kids off our hands now, I've never been so well off. And with vegetables so cheap in the shops, who needs to grow their own? I can make better use of my spare time.'

How times change! In a few short, economically disastrous years, the situation has completely reversed. The question nowadays is: can you afford *not* to grow your own? I reckon the answer to that is a resounding *no*. And if you have a garden but don't grow vegetables, you've got to be some sort of nut. . . .

Just look at the facts. It is possible, for example, to grow a couple of hundred or so cauliflowers from one packet of seeds costing around 25p. If you have a freezer, that lot will keep you and your family in caulies for twelve months. And you don't need me to tell you how much 200 cauliflowers would cost if you bought them from a greengrocer.

The same goes for all other vegetables – everything from brussels and beetroot to parsnips and peppers. Grow 'em right and store them properly, and you've just got to be quids in.

OK, growing vegetables is a time-consuming job. You may have to give up your Saturday afternoon excursion to the football match and probably put an end to the after-lunch catnap in

front of the telly on Sundays. Putting your feet up in the evening when you come home from work will become an occasional rather than a regular habit.

Gardening can be a tough and uncomfortable job too. Occasionally you'll get soaked to the skin as you struggle in the worst of weather to meet the deadline for sowing or planting a particular crop. And you'll have to learn to live with backache after wielding a spade in what can be very stubborn soil. Broken nails, blisters, nasty little cuts – after a few weeks, you could be joining the ranks of the walking wounded. Or you might misdirect the garden fork and spear your foot instead of the soil–in which case you won't be walking anywhere.

Yes, there may be times when you'll wish you'd never started it all. But you'll come through smiling. I've found that saving money (and it could run into three figures a year) puts a grin on the faces of the most stolid of folk. And of course I've exaggerated the dangers – at least, I hope I have! – and it's most unlikely you'll be smiling at your success through a swathe of bandages.

Saving cash isn't the only facet of vegetable gardening that will have you smiling with contentment. Simply growing your own produce will also give you a tremendous kick. Nothing in gardening quite matches the joy and satisfaction of harvesting the first crops from the veg patch. When you pick, for example, the first of the young, tender runner beans, you'll ask yourself 'Did I *really* grow these myself?' And no one, but no one, is going to deny you a few dizzy moments of big-headedness. These successes, and let's hope they come one after the other in rapid succession, will keep you going.

Another important reason for growing your own is that you can choose the varieties you and your family like best. With some vegetables, there are a dozen or more different varieties to choose from – and most of them have an individual taste. So you can have great fun experimenting to find the one that most appeals to your family's tastebuds.

Coupled with this taste business, growing your own also means that *you* govern what chemicals are used in their culture. Some experts believe that certain chemicals used in the commercial growing of crops leave residues in vegetables or fruit that can, over time, have a harmful effect on humans. If you sympathise with this view, then growing your own is one way of making sure that the vegetables your family eats are free of any chemical traces.

The actual methods of growing vegetables are, of course, covered in great detail in this book. You'll find it all comparatively easy once you know how. There is also a chapter telling you how to freeze vegetables, because, without a doubt, the biggest boon to home vegetable growing in the past few years has been the advent of home freezers. These enable you keep your produce for long periods rather than throwing or giving away excess crops. So the message is simple: if you're going to get a veg patch, get a freezer too.

Finally, I must return to my friend who turned his vegetable plot into a lawn in 1970. Yes, you've guessed it – nagging inflation finally caught up with him as it did with the rest of us, and the lawn is now a veg patch again! But it wasn't all a complete waste of time. When he dug up the lawn, he carefully stacked the turves upside down and, within twelve months, these had degenerated into a most beautiful compost.

Peter Peskett

Planning and Preparation

The first thing to decide is how much of your garden you want to devote to vegetables. Several different factors will influence this decision.

1 The size of your family. The fewer people you have to grow for, the smaller the plot can be.

2 What your family likes to eat. For example, you would need a much larger plot for a family partial to potatoes and a regular supply of greenstuff than for a family not keen on one or both of these crops.

3 How much time you've got. Vegetable gardening can be a time-consuming pursuit, so if your spare time is at a premium, don't create a massive plot.

4 The overall size of the garden. Assuming that most people want to retain the ornamental and decorative aspect of their garden, it's wise to restrict the veg plot to no more than one-third of the overall garden area.

So having decided, roughly, what size the veg plot is going to be, the next job is to work out the best spot for it in the garden. A vegetable patch is not the most attractive of sights, so most of us like to tuck it away behind a hedge or screen of some type so that it is not visible from the house.

But be careful. The plot needs to be in a fairly sunny position and within reach, by hosepipe, of a water point.

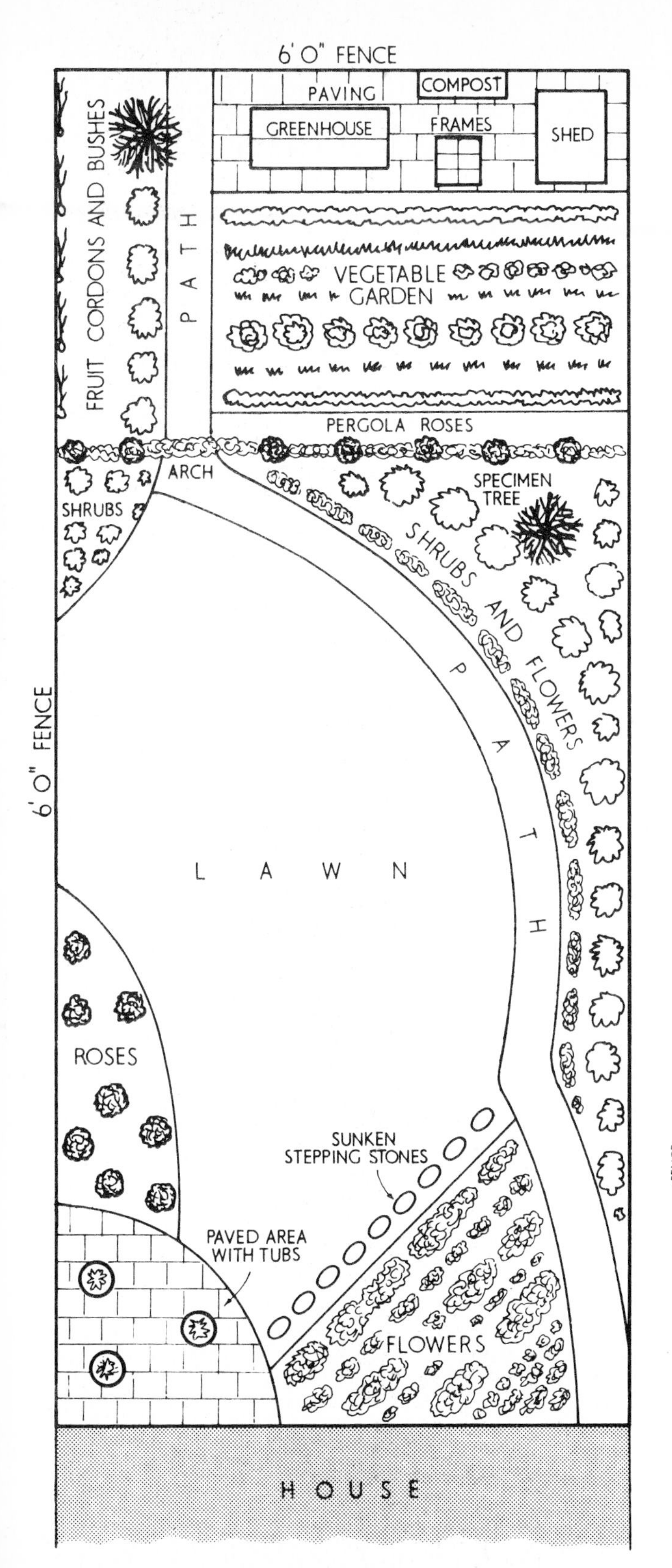

Plot 1

The veg plot has been created at the bottom of this narrow garden and is screened from the house and ornamental section of the garden by a pergola decked with roses. The greenhouse, shed, frames and compost heap have been sited conveniently close to the vegetables.

Plot 2

The problem with this garden is that it is wider than it is long. The site chosen for the veg plot is by no means ideal because the house casts a shadow over it most of the day. But, bearing in mind that the garden has little depth and that the family did not want the vegetables seen from the house, the choice is a satisfactory compromise. Again, the greenhouse, shed, frame and compost bins are close to the vegetables.

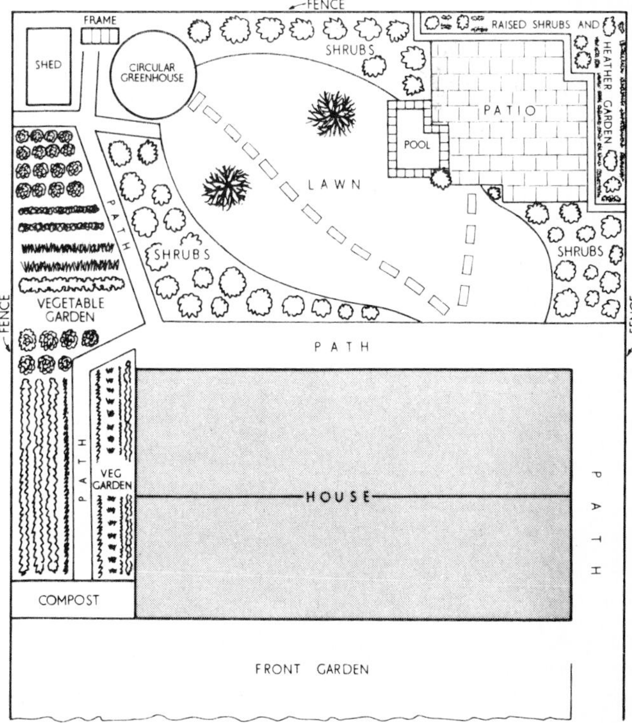

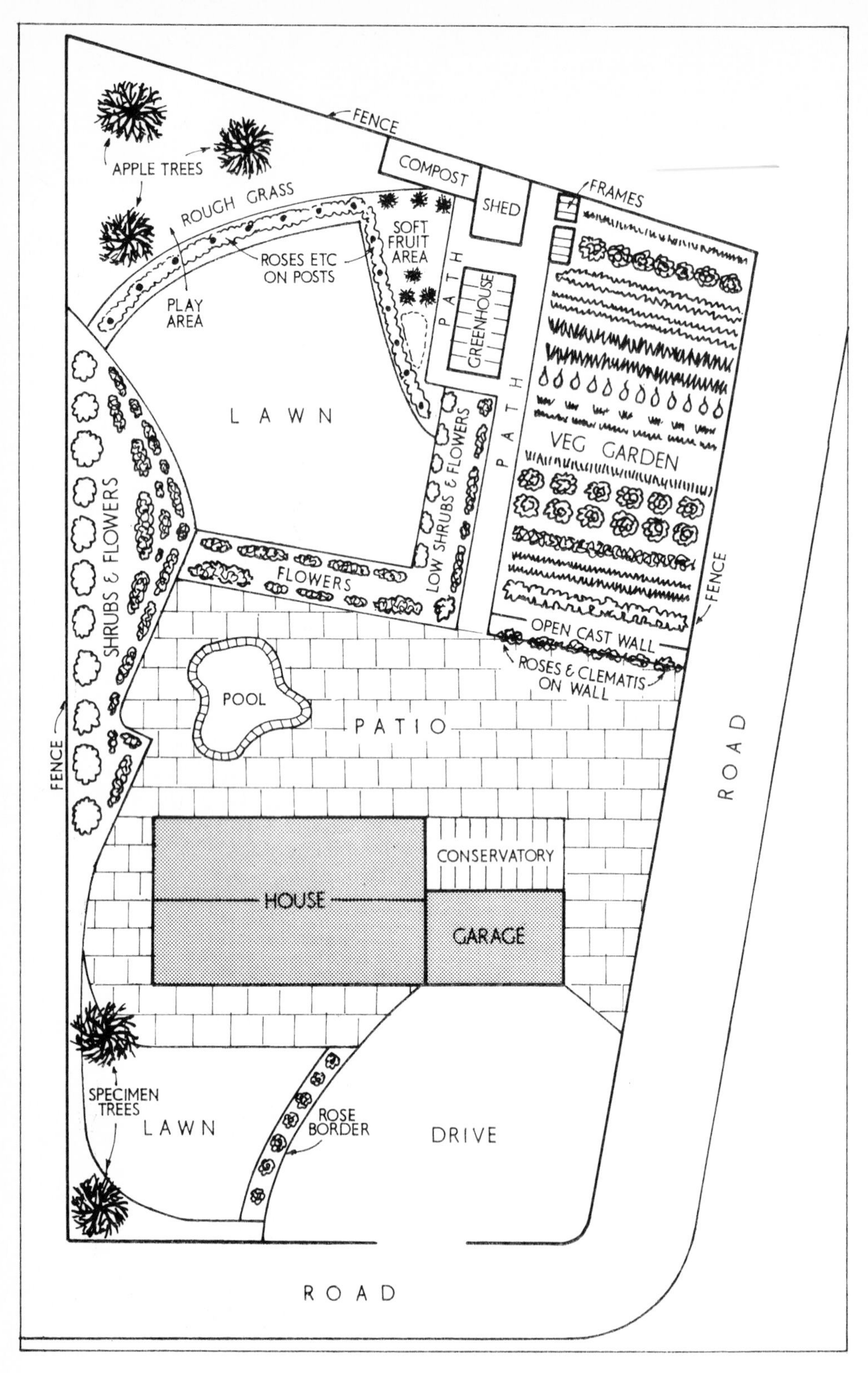

Plot 3

An open-cast wall decorated with roses and clematis screens the large veg plot from the house and patio in this garden. Even though the veg patch is big enough to keep a family of four in fresh vegetables all year round, the overall impression of the garden is decorative rather than productive. That's the ideal to aim for.

Rotation

It has always been considered good practice to keep the different families of vegetables on the move around the veg plot.

There are several reasons for this, the most often quoted being that if the cabbage family is grown in the same place for too long, a build-up of club-root disease is likely.

The possibility applies, in fact, to other diseases: the root-fungus troubles of the onion and shallot family, for instance, and fusarium in peas.

But as well as disease, pests that attack one group in particular are encouraged by repeated sowing or planting of the same crop; possibly the most destructive of these pests is eelworm in potatoes.

There are other considerations too. The different groups get their food from the soil in different ways, and take it or leave it in different quantities. Shallow-rooted things feed on the top 2–3in (5–8cm). Parsnips and carrots reach down into the bottom layers. Brussels sprouts and all the cabbage family drain the soil of nitrogen, and peas and beans leave it behind after they're gone.

The clever gardener takes advantage of all the plants' likes and dislikes. He sees that carrots and parsnips go on ground that was well dug and manured the year before, and that, because his cabbages have to be moved anyway, the patch they are going on gets the liming in that particular year.

And so the merry-go-round of crop rotation goes on. It may not be as practicable in the small garden as on the allotment, or as for the commercial grower, but the principles must always be borne in mind, and acted on as strictly as possible.

These are the families of vegetables:

Chenopodiaceae – Beetroot, spinach.

Compositae – Artichoke (globe and Jerusalem), lettuce.

Cruciferae – Broccoli, brussels sprout, cabbage, cauliflower, kale, savoy, swede, turnip.

Cucurbitacae – Cucumber, marrow.

Leguminosae – Broad bean, French bean, runner bean, pea.

Liliaceae – Asparagus, capsicum, potato, tomato.

Umbelliferae – Carrot, celery, parsley, parsnip.

Vegetables from the same groups should not immediately follow each other in any rotation plan.

This is a suggested rotation plan for the main vegetables in the first year. Divide the plot into three sections and crop as follows.

Section 1
For root vegetables: carrots, parsnips, beetroot. No fresh manure. Anything added must be of a fine texture – peat, leafmould, mushroom compost, etc. Rake a balanced fertiliser into the surface a week or so before sowing the seeds.

Section 2
For the brassicas: cabbage, cauliflowers, brussels, etc, and for the peas and beans. Manure or compost dug in during the autumn. Limed in the winter, and balanced fertiliser raked in in the spring. Any ground vacant before or after a crop can be used for salads.

Section 3
For the potatoes, early and late. Any manure or compost dug in during the autumn or put in the trenches at planting time. No lime. Plant leeks when early potatoes are dug. Onions (seeds or sets) can go on this plot, or can be given a bed which will be permanently used for them.

In the second year, move the crops and plots round to read 3–1–2, and in the third year to 2–3–1.

Tools

In the veg garden, using poor tools not only shows in rough-shod work that doesn't please the eye, but it can be the cause of poor growth, damage and disease in plants. For example, a slick, sharp spade is essential to ensure a good turnover of the soil; without this, unburied weeds will always be beating the crops.

And this is only the effect on the garden. What will bad tools do for the gardener? They will almost certainly give him blisters on his hands, they'll give him backache, and they'll definitely cost him time, because there's nothing like the right tool in good nick for getting on with the job.

Yes, you'll say, but look at the price of the best tools. Well, look at the price of the worst if it comes to that! Taking everything into consideration, a bad tool will cost you more in the end.

The plan must be, if you are just starting a veg garden, to buy just the basic tools, the least you can manage with. Buy the best, be selective, and look for good workmanship and a good finish.

What then, are the basic tools? What must you have, and what can you manage without, at least for a time?

You'll want a spade and you'll want a fork, although if absolutely necessary you can manage without one or the other for a season. You can, at a pinch, dig with a fork and you can shovel weeds or manure with a spade.

Modern stainless steel or chrome spades and forks are marvellous tools. Once you've picked one up, you'll never be satisfied with anything less.

So, too, with hoes. There are Dutch hoes that you push, drag hoes that you pull. Buy the Dutch hoe first; it's the one garden tool no one can do without. The drag hoe can come later.

Plastic-covered steel handles, rubber hand-grips and unorthodox but effective blade-shapes are features to look for.

The best cutting tools are masterpieces. You'll always want a pair of secateurs. The open-spring type has virtually disappeared (thank goodness), and modern types have replaceable parts and self-cleaning blades.

An iron-toothed rake is essential in the veg garden for raking down the soil, and a strong garden line on metal pegs is a must. A trowel is essential too. Some things will go in with a dibber made out of an old spade or fork handle, but you can't do without a trowel in the end.

These things, then, could get you through.

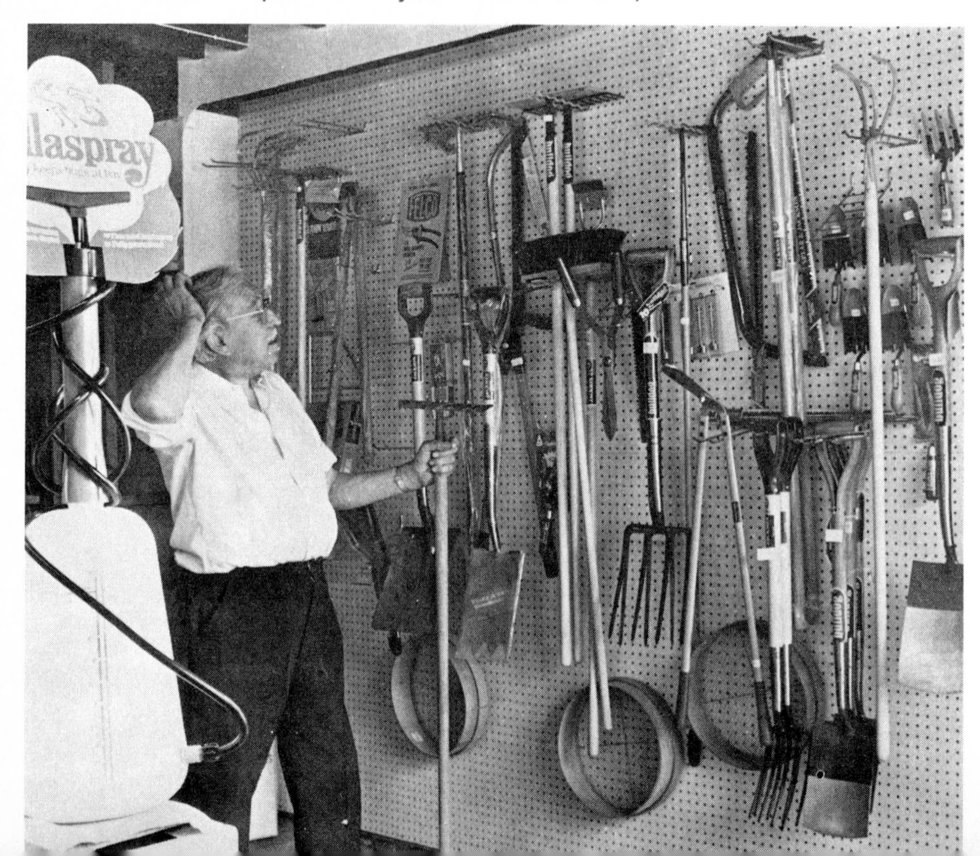

Yes, deciding what tools to buy can be a head-scratching exercise. But whatever you do, make sure you buy the tools that are essential, and go for quality. You'll save a lot of money in the long term.

Digging

We dig mainly to keep the ground in a good mechanical condition. This helps the roots of plants to spread around as they look for food, but it also helps to unlock those foods and make them available.

It allows moisture, air and light to penetrate, and the all-important soil bacteria are set to work. And, of course, the deeper we dig, the more soil gets the benefit of these reactions.

It is the top 9–10in (23–26cm), known as the top spit, that is the most fertile because of its constant exposure, and this top soil must always be kept at the top.

But deeper digging and cultivation bring the lower layers into use, tapping plant foods that may be underneath, improving drainage, and extending the distance that roots can run.

Ordinary digging – that is just turning over the top soil one spade's depth – is sufficient on most ground four years out of five. On light sandy soils, where the drainage may already be too free, it might pay never to dig any deeper. But on heavy ground, a hard layer develops just beyond where the spade reaches, and particularly when it is first dug, this layer needs breaking up.

Once this has been done all over the garden, in subsequent years digging a trench two spits deep for such crops as runner beans and celery, and siting these in different places every year, can be enough. No other double digging is then necessary.

Because exposing the soil to the effects of wind, rain, snow and frost is the best possible way of improving its texture, the main bout of digging is best done in the autumn and early winter.

Frost helps to break up clay and take some of the stickiness out of it. Snow and rain over a period bring minerals from the air, and wind aerates it.

All this puts it in just the right condition for seed sowing and planting when the time comes.

If digging is left until the spring, it is difficult, particularly on heavy ground, to break up the lumps, and seed sowing may be impossible at the right time. The weather will do this job if it is

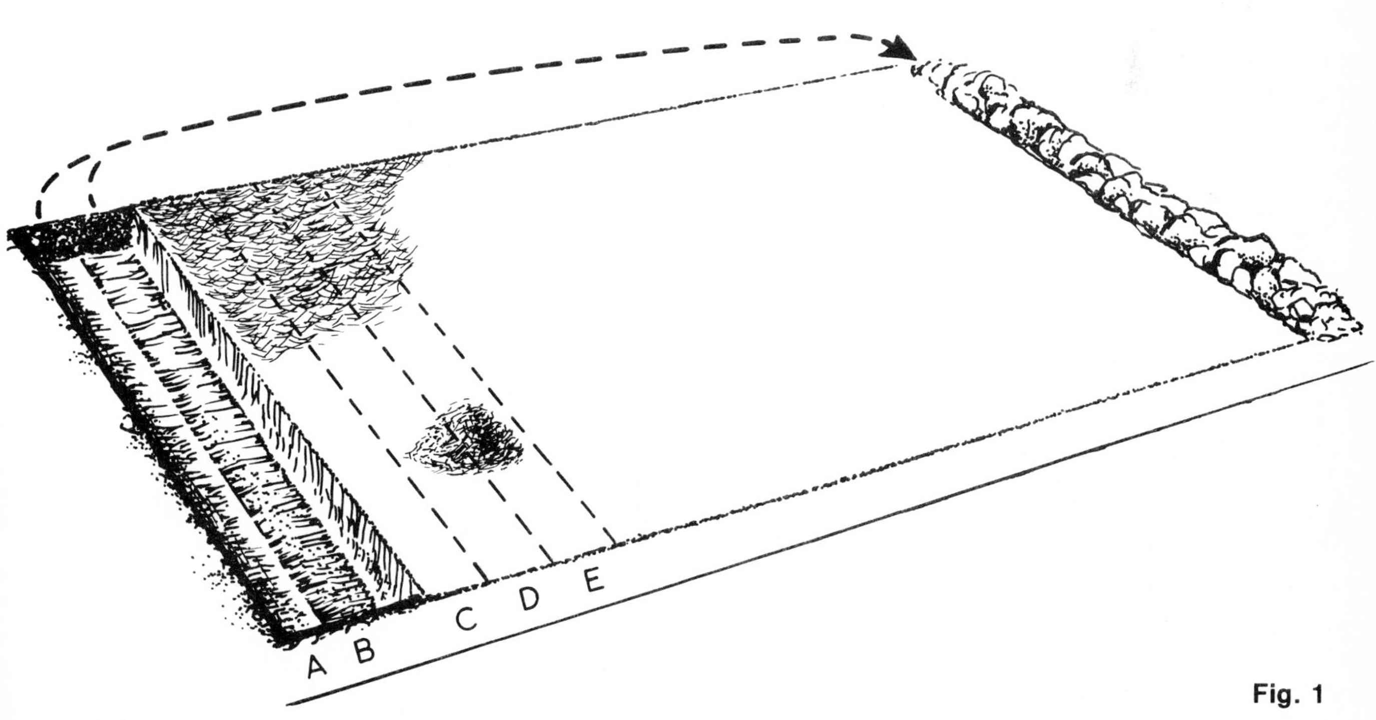

Fig. 1

given the chance. The rougher the surface is left in autumn and winter digging, the more soil is exposed and the greater the benefit.

For spring digging the advice must be to break up the lumps as you go along, but not for early digging. Leave it rough and let the weather do the work, and the heavier the soil, the more important this advice is.

There is no way out of digging unless you have a patch big enough and open enough to be mechanically ploughed and cultivated. Even then, somewhere along the line there will be times when the spade or the fork will have to be used.

A fork is lighter than a spade, and on heavy soil does just as good a job. But on a light soil a spade is best, because a fork runs through it rather than turning it over.

Whichever you dig with, spade or fork, the job is much easier if the tool suits the user for size and weight. Always buy the best you can afford. Good tools are an asset, poor ones a liability.

In practice you'll find that you need both a spade and a fork. Moving manure or compost with a spade is not the most satisfying of operations, and chopping roots or digging a trench with a fork is difficult!

An open trench is essential for good digging. The soil from the first two trenches, A and B, is taken to the far end of the patch (Figure 1, page 11). This soil fills in the end trench when the patch is finished.

The fertility of new ground is greatly improved if the bottom of each trench is forked over and some compost or manure dug in. Do this by getting down into the trench and working from one end to the other.

Manure can be spread on top, or it may be more convenient to leave it in heaps and shovel it along each trench as digging proceeds.

Digging starts by turning spit C over on to A, making sure that weeds are well buried. D then goes on to B, E on to C and so on. It is important to keep a trench clear between the dug and undug soil.

If you haven't got a wheelbarrow, do it as shown in Figure 2.

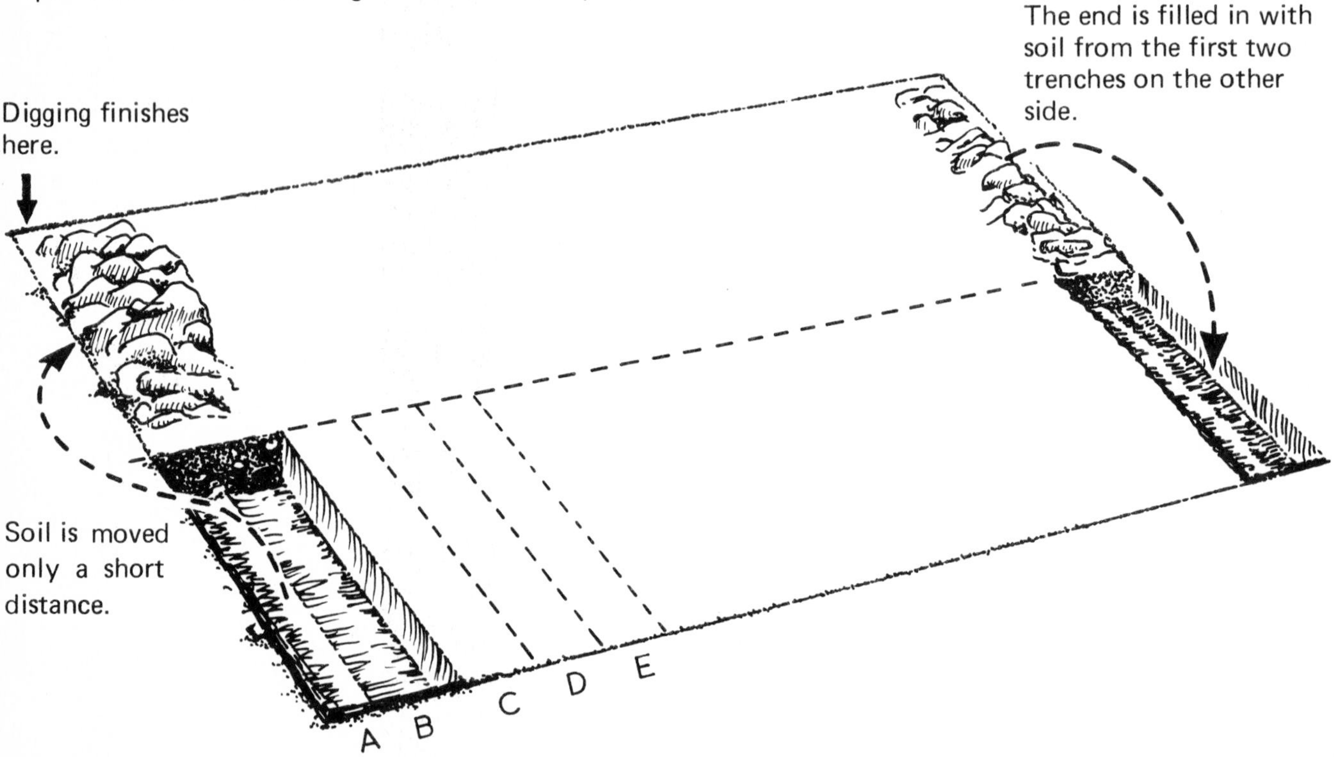

The end is filled in with soil from the first two trenches on the other side.

Digging finishes here.

Soil is moved only a short distance.

A B C D E

If it is not convenient to take soil from one end of the patch to the other, divide down the centre with an imaginary line and dig half at a time.

Fig. 2

Composting

A compost heap will help with the manuring of a garden, but it must not be expected to do everything.

For instance, the waste from a veg patch is never enough on its own to re-manure the same area of ground. And it's far better to use what you have generously in the places you consider most important rather than spreading it around thinly.

On the other hand, if you have a fair supply of lawn mowings and leaves, these – plus normal garden and kitchen waste – might, if intelligently composted and used, be enough to keep the average veg plot going.

Even then, compost on its own rarely supplies everything the vegetable garden needs. It will improve the water-holding of light soils, help the drainage on heavy soils, and improve the structure and texture of any soil. But, if the ground is naturally poor and short of plant foods, something else must be added. Nitrogen, phosphates and potash are the main plant foods, and it is these that are needed. If a balanced fertiliser is raked into the surface of well-composted ground, it will grow almost anything.

A container of some sort is needed to make compost properly and to keep it in a tidy heap. As well as garden waste, lawn mowings and leaves, anything of vegetable origin which will rot down can be put on the compost heap – including kitchen waste, wool and newspapers.

A compost heap (or container, to keep things really tidy) is a 'must' in every garden with a veg patch. And remember, you can use virtually anything of natural origin to build up your supply of compost.

Manures and fertilisers

The division between manures and fertilisers is not clear cut, but for our purpose manures are organic materials – farmyard manure, of course, compost, leaves, sewage, seaweed, fish meal, bonemeal – anything that has grown and been alive.

Fertilisers are mineral plant foods, the three main ones being sulphate of ammonia, which supplies nitrogen, sulphate of potash, which supplies potash, and superphosphate, which supplies phosphates.

Both organic manures and mineral fertilisers are important for plant growth, but there is a difference.

Manure does two jobs. It improves the structure and physical properties in the soil, and it supplies minerals too, in varying degrees. Fertilisers supply the minerals only, and do nothing at all for the soil physically; in fact they have an adverse effect on it.

Crops can be grown without fertilisers–but they can't be grown without manures.

Nature grows her own crops on fallen leaves and waste animal and vegetable matter, and provides enough for wild plants in natural conditions. But in our gardens, especially the vegetable garden, the ground is over-cropped, great demands are made of it, and the normal natural waste is not enough.

Farmyard manure, peat, leaves, hops, straw and home-made garden compost supply the 'body' and do the physical job admirably, but they cannot give the plants all the minerals they need. This is where the fertilisers come in.

It was known that plants extracted nitrogen from the soil to build up stems and leaves, that they needed phosphates for good root growth, and potash for strength, colour and ripening. By various ways these have been produced as concentrated powders, granules, crystals and liquids that plants can assimilate.

The combination of these with the organic materials, whatever they are, opens up new standards for gardeners.

But this is a danger. Because these bare minerals – 'straight' fertilisers as they are called, or compound fertilisers when they are mixed together – are easy and convenient to use, and because they produce such spectacular results, there is a great temptation to rely on them entirely. The temptation is greater still when farmyard manure is unobtainable, other organics are expensive and the compost heap has run out.

But, if used alone, inorganic fertilisers will gradually destroy the texture of soils.

This has happened in many places in the world; the soil has turned to dust and blown away because the structure of the soil was not maintained. However, there is no doubt that, if used wisely, they are a great help in producing bigger and better crops. The rule must be – no chemical fertilisers unless organic manures have been used first.

Because most vegetables are only temporary residents, we get enough opportunity to dig in manures. If plenty of fresh manure is available, turning this in during the autumn and winter is the best possible treatment.

When the bottom spit is being broken up, it can go in there too. Nothing is lost, either, by spreading any surplus on the surface after digging. The rains take the nutrients into the ground, and this is a particularly good way of using the 'hot' manures from pigs and poultry generally considered stronger than those from horses and cattle.

Materials like peat, leafmould, spent hops, etc, are safer to use for spring and summer digging where crops may be going in almost immediately, and just stirring these into the surface is often enough.

Fertilisers are always used in the spring. Either rake them into the surface a week or two before sowing or planting, or use them as supplementaries around growing plants.

Nitrogen is in particular demand while growth is being made. Leafy plants in particular must have it, and a pinch of sulphate of ammonia per plant, kept off the leaves because it burns, will work wonders for the brassica crops, and such plants as lettuce or spinach.

As a general rule, however, it is safest to apply fertilisers in balanced mixtures. Growmore is one of the best examples. It will help to feed all plants, on the principle that it has everything and if they want it, they can take it.

A closer study of what individual plants need must be made before specific single fertilisers are given. Too much of one thing can cause just as much trouble as not enough – perhaps even more. 'Soft' plants full of nitrogen, for instance, are prone to disease and weather damage. Too much phosphate poisons plants, and a surplus of potash hardens and toughens growth and dwarfs plants.

Soil fertility depends on maintaining a balance, and in striving to maintain that fertility and balance the gardener must be generous – but at the same time very careful.

Digging and manuring

Vegetable plots should be planned and prepared well before the start of the season. It is best to start in the autumn, digging the ground over roughly for the winter weather to break down and manuring where necessary.

1 Double digging and manuring will improve drainage of heavy soils and the water-holding capacity of light land. Start by digging a trench one spit deep and removing the crumbs from the bottom. This soil should be carted to the far end of the plot.

2 Break up the bottom of the trench, at the same time digging in peat, farmyard manure or garden compost. In doing this you will probably turn up a small amount of sub-soil which will eventually increase the depth of fertile soil.

3 Cover the manure with the soil from the next trench, leaving it rough for the winter weather to break down to a fine tilth. The soil you have carted to the end of the plot will be used to fill in the final trench.

4 If you don't get the digging done during the winter, the plot can be single dug in the spring. Manure, provided it is well rotted, can be incorporated in the top spit.

5 Cover the manure with soil from the next trench, breaking down the soil to a fairly fine tilth. Before sowing or planting, dress the soil with a general fertiliser. Consolidate it by systematically treading it, and rake to a fine tilth.

Using lime

Lime is the key to soil fertility, and all plants need it in varying degrees. But keys work both ways, and although the right amount of lime sets plant foods free, too much locks them up and causes all kinds of problems.

Never get into the habit, then, of liming the veg garden indiscriminately. There's a temptation when the digging is done to spread lime all over the surface as a kind of all-powerful sweetener. But it can be doing more harm than good.

The principle of putting lime on the top is right, but first find out how much is already there. The trouble is that you can't tell just by looking at it. Heavy soil seems to cry out for lime, because we know that it helps to break it up.

And the light soils may be thought limey enough, just because they break up easily. But looks are deceiving. Soils of any type can be limey or acid, and although there are pointers which the skilled grower can note, even he can be sure only when he has the results of a soil test.

Not that we all have to be chemists. Plants are very accommodating. A few prefer acid soils, some prefer alkaline, the opposite. But most will grow quite well in neutral soil – one that is neither acid or alkaline.

Where the trouble comes in is that this neutrality is always being affected by various things. Rain washes lime away, and air pollution, the plants we grow, and the manures and fertilisers we use, all sway it one way or another; in time it becomes unbalanced.

A soil test, then, is well worth doing every year, and inexpensive home-testing kits are available at all garden stores.

The procedure is quick and simple enough. A sample is taken from 2–3in (5–8cm) down, and dried and crumbled to dust. A test tube is quarter filled with this, and then filled to the top with a chemical solution. After ten minutes or so the colour will change, and it is then compared with the colours on a chart supplied.

The range is from red, which indicates very acid, through orange to yellow, on to green and further on to bluey-green which is alkaline. What are known as pH numbers accompany the colours, 4.5 at the red end and 7.5 at the blue. Green is neutral at about 7.

It is important, of course, to get representative samples of soil, or to make several tests at different spots.

Most vegetables are happy with a pH number between 6 and 7. All the cabbage family have a preference for the limey end of this range, and potatoes like the other end.

For practical purposes then, and considering that the tendency is always towards the ground losing lime, a soil registering around neutral, or just under, should be left as it is for potatoes, and limed for brassicas. Rotation from year to year keeps this balance, and the other crops, a fairly tolerant lot, are quite content to share this arrangement.

It is always easy to add lime, far more difficult to take it away. A naturally limey soil will generally grow good brassicas if it is heavily manured, but potatoes in the same ground will often be poor, and at the least have scab disease.

It may well be worth forgetting potatoes for a year or two on such ground, until the organic additions begin to tell. If you are determined to grow them, manuring, plus a lining of peat immediately in contact with the tubers when they are planted, and sulphate of ammonia as a fertiliser applied just before earthing up, will help.

One thing more. If you are liming ground, don't walk backwards and forwards on the soil spreading it. Never walk on dug ground unless you have to. Lime is best spread on the top when the digging is done, but do it one day when the surface is frozen hard and your footprints make no impression.

Colour
Beetroot 'Detroit Little Ball' – bred specially for use late in the year and recommended when globe-shaped roots are preferred for table use to the long variety of beet often associated with winter use (Picture: Ian and Stuart Unwin)

Seeds and plants

Because they don't transplant very well, some vegetables are best sown directly where they are to grow and mature, the seeds being sprinkled into drills and the surplus removed when 1–2in (2.5–5cm) high, to leave single specimens with the required room to grow.

Carrots, parsnips and beetroot come into this category, and so for these and a few others you have to obtain and sow seeds.

But some things transplant very well (in fact, seem to benefit by being moved), and so we can buy these as plants if we wish.

The cabbage family is the prime example. Plants are always available at garden centres, etc, at the right planting times.

Many gardeners find it more convenient to buy enough plants for a row of brussels sprouts, say, across their patch, than to buy and sow a packet of seeds which inevitably produce more plants than are needed. Often the surplus is wasted and, of course, they need ground and time and effort to produce. The cost may not be of any consequence: a packet of seeds and a dozen or two plants would cost around the same.

A list, then, of the vegetables that are always available as plants will not come amiss, along with the times of planting – which, of course, are the times to be looking for them in the shops and garden centres.

Asparagus
Crowns, as they are called, are planted in April. Look for them at that time or order them from a supplier in advance.

Artichokes, globe
Obtainable as small offsets in April.

Colour
Above Radish 'Saxa' – no, you don't need to add salt to give it taste! Excellent for sowing early in the season and it's quick to mature (Picture: Ian and Stuart Unwin)

Below Onion 'Rijnsburger' – sounds like something you grill and eat sandwiched in a bun, but this is really a very good onion. It has a strong skin and is a good keeper (Picture: Ian and Stuart Unwin)

Artichokes, Jerusalem
Tubers to be planted in February/March.

Beans, broad
Not commonly offered for sale, but available, if at all, in March.

Beans, runner
Can't be planted until frosts have gone. On sale for a short period from mid-May to early June.

Broccoli, sprouting
Look for these in June.

Brussels sprouts
Plants started in greenhouses are offered in March/April. Expensive, but have certain advantages. Later plants from outside sowings available in May/June.

Cabbages and cauliflowers
As brussels sprouts.

Capsicum (peppers)
For inside planting, plants ready from March onwards. For outside, early June.

Celery
Available in June for a short period.

Cucumber
For inside planting March onwards. For cold frames, April/May. Outdoor varieties in June.

Leeks
Early plants not offered as a rule, but available from June onwards.

Lettuce
Plants always available from March until June.

Marrows
Single plants in pots always offered in late May and June.

Melons
For growing inside offered from March onwards.

Onions
Little onions known as 'sets' are offered all winter; planting time is April. Onion plants for growing big onions, generally for exhibition, are available from specialist growers in April/May.

Shallots
Buy during the winter, plant in March.

Sweet corn
Single plants in pots available from mid-May to mid-June.

Tomatoes
For planting inside, early plants available in March. For cold houses, from mid-April onwards. For outside, from mid-May onwards.

The keen gardener, however, often sows his own seeds and raises his own plants of almost everything and there are several advantages in doing this.

The first is that he will be able to pick and choose his varieties. In a catalogue, for instance, or on a seed rack in the garden centre, there will be the choice of perhaps a dozen or more tomato varieties. If buying plants, the choice may be limited to only one or two.

The same applies to the brassicas. Often it is difficult to discover the name of the cabbage or the brussels plants you buy, and it has been known for supposed cabbages to turn out as brussels anyway!

No such trouble with seeds. Early Snowball you know will produce early cauliflowers. Late Giant will produce them late. You will find that you prefer the flavour of some kinds to others.

Another advantage of raising your own is that your plants are there just when you want them, and they can be transplanted from the seed box or the seed bed without having to spend withering hours out of the ground.

Buying seeds

There are several ways of buying seeds. Many of the local allotment and gardening societies make bulk purchases for their members and are able to offer them at discount prices.

A particular advantage of this is that the old hands of the society know the varieties suitable for their own areas, and their advice is always worth listening to.

If you like to study and find things out for yourself, acquire as many mail order catalogues as possible. These are mines of information; it can be safely assumed that anyone who publishes and distributes at great expense a good catalogue, can be relied on to supply good seeds.

Most of the top firms that produce catalogues and sell by mail order also sell through direct retail outlets, although the full range of seeds and varieties may not always be available on demand.

There is nothing at all against obtaining seeds 'off the peg', as it were, from a shop or a supermarket, if you are armed with the right kind of knowledge. If, for example, you are not sure about lettuce and don't bother to read what the packet says, it is all too easy for you to come away with a packet of greenhouse lettuce which is not at all suitable for growing outside.

Or you could find yourself with a bush tomato instead of an upright grower for the greenhouse.

There are all kinds of pitfalls, so if you are buying like this do a bit of homework first. Be careful to read and digest the small print – and often it is too small – on the packet.

The term 'F1 hybrid' may baffle some buyers unnecessarily, and pelleted seeds are another complication. Both are more expensive than 'ordinary' seeds.

F1 hybrids are renowned for producing extremely uniform results and are always reliable.

Pelleted seeds are of value when sowing crops that have to be thinned out, because they can be easily spaced out in the drills at the right distance apart. The drawback is that their coating is an additional slight obstacle to good germination if the conditions are not just right.

The big question that hangs over all seed buying is the quantity in the packet. An ounce of seed never changes, of course, nor does a pint or a half-pint. But not many amateur gardeners need such quantities.

Packet size is nothing to go by, and nor in these years of inflation are last year's prices. With some things it is possible to feel and estimate quantities, but even then the beginner is only guessing.

Popular Vegetables

Artichoke, globe

This is quite an ornamental perennial plant that is grown for its globe-like flower-heads. These are cut and eaten while they are still buds. Two or three plants are enough for the average garden. They grow around 4ft (1.2m) high and should be planted at least 30in (75cm) apart.

Culture
Likes a rich soil and the old plants should be mulched every year with a layer of manure over the root area. Liquid fertilisers will help to swell the flower buds. The crowns are best protected with straw or litter during January and February, pulling it away when growth starts in March and thinning out the shoots to the best two or three. Plants deteriorate after three or four years and it's always best to have new ones coming along.

Propagation
The suckers removed in March/April will make new plants. They can be set direct in their permanent positions as they root very easily.

Harvesting
First buds are ready in July and after cutting the main one, the side shoots, though smaller, will go on developing. Always cut before the tips of the petals/scales go brown and hard.

Artichoke, Jerusalem

A tall, easy-to-grow plant that will make a 6–8ft (1.8–2.5m) screen, useful to hide the compost heap or similar areas in summer. The potato-like tubers are the parts eaten.

Culture
Will grow almost anywhere but best soil gives best crops. Cut plants down to the ground in the autumn.

Propagation
Tubers saved when digging are replanted in February/March, 12in (30cm) apart and 3in (8cm) deep.

Harvesting
Dig as required from late autumn on through the winter, or lift the whole crop in October/November and store as potatoes.

Diseases and pests
Slugs and wireworms will eat into the tubers. Use slug pellets and soil insecticides.

Asparagus

A perennial, grown in a permanent 'bed'. The young shoots are cut when 4–6in (10–15cm) above soil level. Cutting lasts about six weeks from an established bed. Thirty to fifty plants are needed to give a worth-while crop.

Culture
Never try to grow asparagus in ground where there are perennial weeds such as bindweed, couch grass, ground elder, etc. For a single row, dig and manure a trench as for runner beans, leaving the surface 6in (15cm) below the level on either side. Set plants 15in (38cm) apart along row and cover with 2–3in (5–8cm) of soil. Hoeing and subsequent earthing-up will gradually fill the trench. A general balanced fertiliser at 2oz (60gm) a yard run should be given in spring, and a mulch of manure in late June and July.

Propagation
Asparagus can be grown from seed, sown in spring along the trench and thinned out. But to save time, it is better to buy one- or two-year-old plants, called crowns, to set out in April.

Harvesting
No shoots must be cut the first year, very few the second year. Plants must be four years old before cutting can be continuous – from April to mid-June. Always cut below soil level and go over the bed every day during the cutting period.

Pests
Asparagus beetle eats the feathery foliage in June, and this affects the crop the following year. Spray with derris in late May.

Aubergines

Sometimes called egg plants, these belong to the same family as tomatoes and like almost exactly the same conditions. In a greenhouse they will produce up to a dozen fruits per plant; outside, about half that number.

Culture
Plants are raised from seed, as for tomatoes, and planted in a warm greenhouse in March, in frames or under cloches in May, or outside in a warm protected spot in early June. They do well in growing bags set against a south-facing wall or fence. Pinch out tips when 6–8in (15–20cm) high to induce branching, but thin branches out to three or four, to limit the number of fruits, and pinch tips off when fruit starts to swell. Keep well watered and liquid-fed.

Propagation
Seed sown in greenhouses at 60°F (15°C) in February or March for growing inside. Sow at the same temperature in March/April for cloches and frames, and in April for growing outside.

Harvesting
Cut with secateurs to avoid damage to plant. If left on plants too long, the flavour and texture deteriorates.

Pests
Spray regularly over and under the leaves with clear water to deter red spider.

Beans, broad

Easy to grow, quite hardy, but with a limited appeal. They have to be picked and used before they get old, but freeze well.

Culture
Not very demanding regarding soil, but on light soils need plenty of manure or compost to hold moisture. Pinch out the tops when in full flower to discourage black fly.

Propagation
Seed of the longpod varieties can be sown in October/November for early crops. Windsor varieties should be sown in February/March. Set 3in (8cm) deep, each side of a line 9in (25cm) apart. Rows go 2ft (60cm) apart.

Harvesting
Pick when beans are formed inside the pod, before they go hard.

Pest and diseases
Black fly is the only pest. Chocolate spot causes leaves to go brown; spray with fungicide at the first sign of brown spots.

Beans, dwarf

Two types of these have been developed. Some are grown and eaten whole as runner beans, others are grown for shelling like peas. They are convenient and easy to grow, and are earlier to crop than runners. Excellent for freezing.

Culture
An open sunny site in fertile soil produces the best crops. They will also do well in window boxes, tubs, etc, and under cloches; they can be grown in pots or growing bags in the greenhouse for early pickings in exposed places. A string or other support is advisable along the sides of the rows.

Propagation
Sow outside in early to mid-May – and again in June for succession. Space seeds 3in (8cm) apart in rows 15in (40cm) apart. Sow in February or March under glass for growing in pots.

Harvesting
Pick the pod varieties regularly when young. Those for shelling must be ripe.

Pests
Red spider should be kept from plants under glass by syringing regularly with water. Black fly and slugs are the most likely pests outside.

Beans, runner

One of the most prolific of vegetables for summer and autumn and very suitable for freezing.

Culture
Best grown on 6ft (2m) supports of net string or sticks, but can also be grown as dwarfs, continually pinching out the ends of the shoots. Must have a moisture-retaining soil, and they like plenty of organic matter – compost, manure, etc – at their roots. Watering will increase crop as long as once started it is not neglected. Overhead spraying will help flowers to 'set'.

Propagation
If seed is to be sown in open ground, early May is about the earliest it can be risked. Plants will not stand any frost. If to be started in pots in the greenhouse or frame, sow end of April, and plant out towards end of May.

Harvesting
Pick often and regularly while the beans are young.

Pests
Red spider, slugs and black fly (see Beans, dwarf).

Beetroot

Very popular vegetable for pulling and using when young and small or can be lifted at the end of the season and stored in dry peat or sand for use throughout the winter. There are globe and long varieties. Globe are more convenient to use.

Culture
Will grow in most soils, but prefers light loams and open sunny situations. Needs to be grown quickly or roots will be tough.

Propagation
Seeds are sown in 1in (2–3cm) deep drills in rows 1ft (30cm) apart. If to be used young, thin seedlings to 2–3in (5–8cm) apart. If for storing, thin to 6in (15cm). Sow in April and July for succession.

Harvesting
Pull first when big as golf balls. Tennis-ball size is about right for storing. Roots must not be damaged or they will 'bleed'. Twist leaves off rather than cut.

Pests
Flea beetle will sometimes attack the seedlings as they come through. Dust with derris as a precaution.

Broccoli

The heading types of these are now called winter cauliflowers. Broccoli are the types that produce white or purple sprouting growths in the spring, after standing through the winter from a summer planting. They provide 'greens' at a time when most others are scarce (March, April, May).

Culture
Plants are set out in June and July and can often follow early harvested crops, such as early potatoes, peas, lettuce, etc. They must not be grown too 'soft' with nitrogenous fertilisers or winter damage may result.

Popagation
Seeds are sown ½in (13mm) deep in a seed bed in April and May, and the plants set out when 6in (15cm) or so high, around 2ft (60cm) apart all ways. They may need watering in.

Harvesting
Pick the young shoots regularly as they appear. If allowed to go to flower they become tough and stringy.

Pests
Slugs may attack young plants, and pigeons are a pest in winter in some districts. Usual brassica troubles of club root, cabbage root fly, aphis and caterpillars must be guarded against.

Brussels sprouts

These are the mainstay of the winter 'greens'. They are quite hardy and can be picked as they are needed from October to March. Excellent for freezing when there is a surplus.

Culture
They like a rich firm soil, sweetened with lime and a long season of growth. The earlier the plants are established in their final positions the better; plantings made after June will not produce full-size plants and a big crop. The best planting distance is 30in (75cm) each way. Radish or lettuce can be sown between as catch crops.

Propagation
Seeds can be started in a warm greenhouse in February, pricked out in boxes and hardened off in a cold frame for planting out in May. Or they can be sown outside in a seed bed in March for planting when 6in (15cm) high.

Harvesting
Pick as needed, working up from the bottom of the plant and removing yellowing leaves.

Pests
As all brassicas.

Cabbage

There are three main types of cabbage: spring, summer and winter. Spring are planted in autumn, to stand through the winter for use in March, April and May. Summer are planted from March to June, for use from June to September. Winter are planted in June, for use from October to March.

Culture
Like all brassicas, they need rich soil containing some lime. Planting distances must suit the variety, 15–24in (38–60cm) between plants, 18in (45cm) between rows. Spring cabbage plants can be set 9in (23cm) apart, cutting every other one early in the season as 'spring greens' and leaving others to heart.

Propagation
Spring cabbage seeds are sown in late July or early August in a seed bed, and transplanted in September/October to permanent positions. Summer cabbage may be started in greenhouse as brussels, using quick-maturing varieties which heart up in June or July, or they may be sown outside in March, and transplanted when 6in (15cm) high for use in July/August/September. Winter cabbage seeds are sown outside in April/May for transplanting in June or July, for use from October onwards.

Harvesting
Cut when hearted, before bursting.

Pests
As all brassicas.

Calabrese

A sprouting broccoli type of vegetable, which crops in the same year as planting. Green shoots are produced in succession, August until November, if continually picked. Excellent for freezing.

Culture
As for all brassicas.

Propagation
Sow in seed bed in April. Transplant 18in (45cm) apart all ways when 6in (15cm) high.

Harvesting
Pick green sprouts as they appear. Pick regularly or flowers will appear and production will stop.

Pests
As for other brassicas.

Cauliflowers

In theory, by selecting the right varieties, cauliflowers can be produced for any time of the year. But much depends on the climate. Many winter varieties are only hardy enough to grow in favoured, mostly southern, districts. Early summer varieties are not easy to grow consistently well.

Culture
Summer varieties in particular must be grown without a check, watering the plants in when transplanted. Rich soil is necessary and liquid fertiliser will help to form good heads. Winter varieties are less demanding but must have good soil, and must be well established in growing positions by the autumn.

Propagation
Seed of May/June maturing varieties is sown in a warmed greenhouse in January or February. Plants are set out, possibly under cloches, in March. For the summer and autumn varieties, seed is sown in March/April in seed beds outside, transplanted when 6in (15cm) high. Winter varieties are sown in May, planted out in June/July.

Harvesting
According to variety. Earliest varieties in May/June, summer and autumn varieties in July/November, winter from December (in favourable districts) to June. Must be cut when ready. Will freeze well.

Pests
As all brassicas, but summer varieties particularly prone to root-fly attack.

Carrots

There is no reason why an all-the-year-round supply of carrots should not be available from a garden with cloches or a cold frame. Quick-growing varieties are pulled and used when small, and maincrop varieties will keep all winter in store.

Culture
Carrots like a light sandy soil, but it must hold moisture. Heavy soils must be well cultivated. Fresh manure will cause roots to fork.

Propagation
Seeds of early-maturing varieties are sown under cloches or in frames in February, and outside in March. Maincrop varieties are sown in April, in ½in (13mm) deep drills, 12in (30cm) apart. These should be thinned to 3–4in (7–10cm) apart. More early varieties are sown in June and July for pulling in bunches until November/December.

Harvesting
Pull early varieties and use as needed. Lift main crops in September/October. Cut off tops and store in boxes of ashes, peat or sand in a garage or similar. Or they can be stood against a wall outside and covered with sand 3–4in (7–10cm) thick.

Pests
Greenfly will infest tops – spray at very first signs. Carrot fly lays eggs around plants in May/June and the maggots bore into roots causing damage and possible plant collapse. Soil insecticides along seed drills at sowing time will help to keep them away.

Celeriac

Commonly known as turnip-rooted celery, which describes it exactly. The root swells and can be lifted and stored through the winter. Use in soups or grated in a salad.

Culture
Must have well-manured, moisture-retaining soil. Set plants out in June 9–12in (23–30cm) apart and keep watered. Take off all side-shoots around central group.

Propagation
Sow seeds in warm greenhouse (50°F or 10°C) in March. Prick out seedlings into boxes, harden off in cold frame and plant out in June.

Harvesting
Pull and use when big enough. Lift and store in sand or peat in October/November.

Pests
As for celery.

Celery

Not an easy crop to grow well. There are two main types: blanching, which have to be wrapped or earthed up to bleach stems, and self-blanching or American green, which have naturally crisp stems. Self-blanching varieties are not hardy and must be used before winter.

Culture
Moisture-retaining soil is essential, with manure or compost incorporated. Blanched celery is often grown in trenches and earthed up as it grows, or can be grown on top of the ground and wrapped to exclude light. Self-blanching are best set 9in (23cm) apart in square blocks. Water is essential in dry periods.

Propagation
As celeriac.

Harvesting
Lift as needed. Pink and red varieties of blanched celery are not harmed by frost.

Pests
Slugs are worst pests. Slug pellets and soot in ground will help. Celery fly tunnels between leaf surfaces. Pick off by hand and spray with malathion.

Chicory

Witloof varieties of chicory make parsnip-like roots which are dug up at the end of the season and started into new growth during winter under cover. The top growth is blanched by excluding light and produces white 'chicons'. A new variety, Crystal Head, needs no blanching, producing lettuce-like hearts in late summer and autumn.

Culture
Witloof varieties are best grown in soil manured the previous year so that good straight roots are produced. Crystal Head must be sown no earlier than late June. It is likely to go to seed if sown before this.

Propagation
Seeds are sown in ½in (13mm) deep drills, 18in (45cm) between rows. Thin Witloof varieties to 6in (15cm) Crystal Head to 12in (30cm).

Harvesting
Dig Witloof roots in October/November, cut off leaves and trim roots. Store in sand. Set five or six roots upright in a 9in (23cm) pot of compost, water and keep completely dark. Cut in approximately four weeks. Cut Crystal Head as they heart.

Cucumbers

There are two types, indoor and outdoor. The indoor must be in a greenhouse or cold frame. Outdoor varieties will grow unprotected outside, but cannot be planted until mid-June.

Culture
Indoor varieties need warm humid conditions, plenty of water and organic matter mixed with loam, or will do well in grow-bags. They must be shaded from strong sunshine and sprayed at least once a day with clear water. Tie the leading shoot to upright cane and pinch out tip when it reaches the top. Cucumbers form on side shoots, and these must be pinched two leaves past the fruit. In frames, pinch out the tip of the plant when 6in (15cm) high, spread shoots to cover frame, and pinch out tips when walls are reached. Take off male flowers, ie those with no immature fruit behind them.

Propagation
Sow seeds of earliest plants in 65°F (18°C), one in a 3in (8cm) pot, in January/February/March. For frames, sow in early May. For outside planting, sow in mid-May.

Harvesting
Cut when large enough before any signs of yellowing.

Pests
Red spider is a pest that only attacks in dry conditions. Regular spraying and humidity will keep it away. White fly are sometimes troublesome, but beware of using some insecticides that are unsuitable for cucumbers.

Kohl rabi

A member of the cabbage family, but has a root that swells and tastes something like a turnip. Quickly goes tough and stringy in dry weather or if allowed to get too old.

Culture
Not fussy about soil as long as it isn't acid.

Propagation
Seeds sown in 1in (2–3cm) deep drills, rows 12–15in (30–38cm) apart. Sow anytime from March until July. Thin seedlings to 6–8in (15–20cm) apart.

Harvesting
Pull and use before roots get old, at ten to twelve weeks. Crops from late sowings can be pulled in October and stored in peat or sand.

Pests
As all brassicas.

Leeks

A useful vegetable because they will stay in the garden unharmed all through the winter and can be dug as they are needed from November until April.

Culture
Like a fairly rich soil, but will grow in most open, well cultivated gardens. Plants about the thickness of a pencil are dropped into holes 6–10in (15–25cm) deep, watering them in but not filling the holes with soil. Rows 15in (38cm) apart. Trimming the ends of the roots and leaves makes them easier to plant.

Propagation
The earlier the plants are set out in the garden the bigger the leeks will be. For the biggest specimens seeds are sown in a warm greenhouse from January onwards, and seedlings pricked out and hardened off for planting in March. For an ordinary crop, sow in seed bed in ½in (13mm) deep drill in March and transplant as soon as big enough.

Harvesting
Dig as needed.

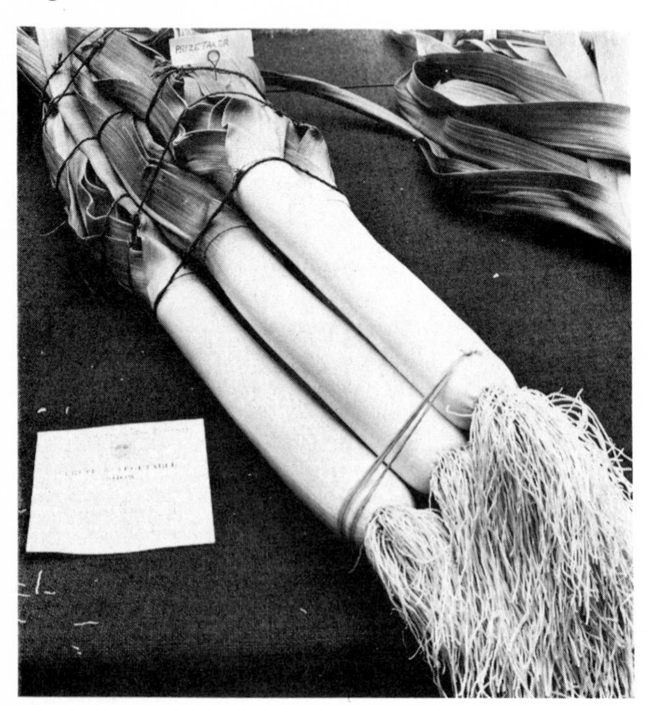

Lettuce

Can be produced from the open garden from May to October. With a greenhouse, frame or cloches, the season can be extended if you use suitable varieties.

Culture
Organic matter, manure, compost, etc, should be in the top 3–4in (8–10cm) of soil, mainly to hold moisture. To make good hearts they must have room to develop, 6–12in (15–30cm) according to variety, and must be in an open, unshaded position.

Propagation
First seeds of the year are sown in warm greenhouse in January/February, pricked out into boxes and planted in cold frames or under cloches in February/March, or outside unprotected from mid-March onwards. First sowings are made outside in March, ½in (13mm) deep drills, rows 12in (30cm) apart. For succession, sow every three weeks. Thin seedlings according to variety. Transplanting seedlings can be done until June. After that throw away, leaving only the plants *in situ*. Continue sowings until mid-August. Sow winter variety in September for standing through winter and using in April.

Harvesting
Lettuce is eatable at any stage, but once hearted up must be watched for running to seed.

Pests
Greenfly, cutworms, root aphis and birds are possible attackers.

Marrows and courgettes

Marrows and courgettes are very much the same, courgettes being varieties of marrows that are bred to produce a lot of smaller fruit rather than a few big ones. They will, however, grow into 'marrows' if they are left. A fast growing crop and very productive if plenty of moisture is available. Bush and trailing types are available.

Culture
Plants are susceptible to frost damage and must not be set out unprotected until early June. They like plenty of organic matter in the soil and will do well in partial shade. Bush types are best for most gardens, but trailers can be grown on top of compost heaps, etc, as a camouflage. Feeding and watering will help to swell fruits.

Propagation
Seeds are sown one in a 3in (8cm) pot in greenhouse or frame in late April or May. Plants are then set out under cloches in late May, or outside unprotected in early June. Alternatively, seeds can be sown direct where they are to grow, 1in (2.5cm) deep in mid-May.

Harvesting
Cut courgettes regularly when they are 4–6in (10–15cm) long. Marrows can be left to grow to full size, but regular cutting gives later fruits more chance.

Pests
Slugs are the worst problem. Sprinkle pellets around each plant.

Melons

Melons grow best in warm, humid glasshouses, but some of the modern varieties are hardier and will do well in cold glasshouses, frames or cloches.

Culture
A mound of well-rotted manure or compost plus soil, with the plant set on top, is best in the greenhouse, or they do well in grow-bags. Train the main stem up a cane, pinch tip when at the top and also pinch tip of side-shoots. Melons form on all side-shoots. Female flowers, those with immature melons behind them, must be fertilised with pollen taken from male flowers. Try to pollinate the whole crop, six, eight or ten melons, on the same day. Spray the whole plant with water daily and feed as fruit swells. Pinch growing point out of plants in frames or cloches when five leaves have been made. Direct shoots to cover growing area and pinch tips again. Pollinate as inside.

Propagation
Sow seeds one in a pot in March/April in a warm greenhouse for greenhouse growing. Sow in May for planting in frames and cloches in June. Cantaloupe types are best for unheated growing. Support fruit on tile or similar to keep off soil.

Harvesting
Sweet smell indicates ripeness, plus a slight softening at stalk end.

Pests
Red spider mite will infest if atmosphere is not kept humid.

Onions

Onions are grown for their bulbs or for use as salad onions. Thinnings from a row being grown for bulbs may be used as salads, but for salads alone it is easier and cheaper to sow a special variety such as White Lisbon. Bulb onions are also grown from 'sets', which are small bulbs produced by specialist growers.

Culture
Well manured and cultivated ground in full light, dug and prepared if possible in the autumn, and top dressed with Growmore or similar, 4oz (100gm) to the square yard, in February/March. Ground must be kept hoed to control weeds.

Propagation
For salads only, sow White Lisbon seeds in ½in (13mm) deep drills, rows 9in (23cm) apart in March and again in May for succession. For big exhibition bulbs sow in a warm greenhouse in January, prick out, harden off and plant out in April. For ordinary bulbs sow in drills 12in (30cm) apart in March and thin seedlings to 4–6in (10–15cm) apart. To provide bulbs in June/July/August, sow Japanese varieties in August and thin out in the spring. Onion sets are planted 9in (23cm) apart in April.

Harvesting
Onions for keeping must be ripe and well dried off. The tops will bend over at the end of the growing season, and after a week or two can be lifted and spread out in sunshine to dry. Clean off tops after a week or so, and store in a dry, cool, airy place.

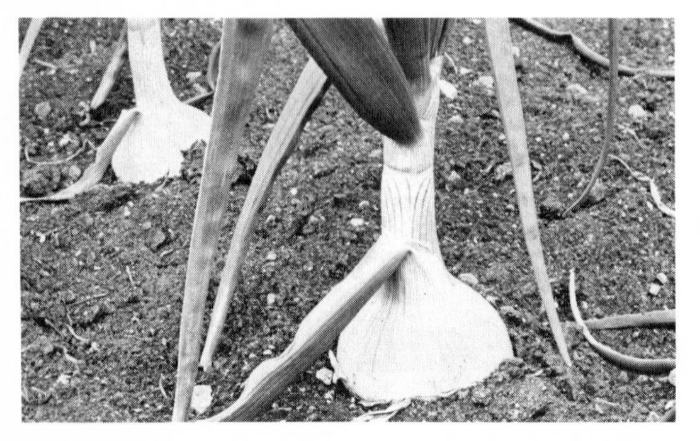

Pests and disease
Use soil insecticides to combat onion fly. Soil can become infected with fungus diseases, which mean that onions have to be grown elsewhere.

Parsnip

A completely hardy vegetable, which can be left in the garden and dug as needed through the winter.

Culture
Best on ground manured for a previous crop, as fresh manure causes forked and distorted roots.

Propagation
Sow seeds in ½in (13mm) deep drills, 15in (38cm) apart in March/April and thin out seedlings to 6in (15cm) apart.

Harvesting
Dig as required.

Diseases
Brown marks, known as canker, sometimes spoil the crop. Avon Resister is a variety that is resistant to this trouble.

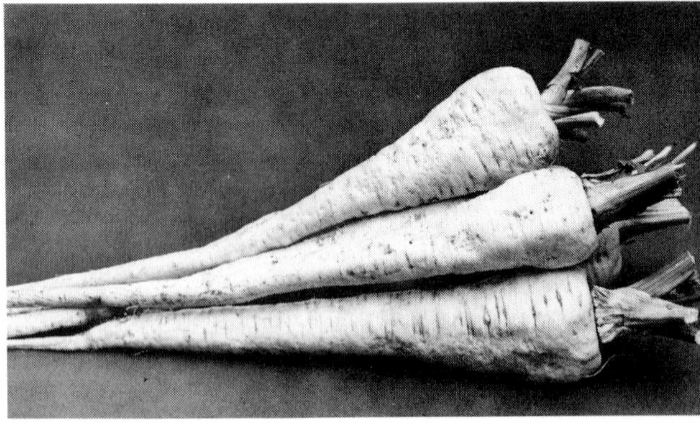

Colour
Carrot 'St Valery' – with its long, tapering roots, this variety is popular with horticultural show exhibitors. Yields are heavy . . . and it tastes good, too! (Picture: Ian and Stuart Unwin)

Overleaf Carrot 'Chantenay' – a nice, crisp, maincrop variety that has broad shoulders and is red throughout. Generally produces high yields (Picture: Ian and Stuart Unwin)

Peas

There are two ways of growing successive crops of peas. A single maincrop variety can be sown at three-week intervals from March to June. Or a range of varieties, earlies, maincrop and lates, can be sown all at the same time in March/April. Earlies take eleven to twelve weeks from sowing to picking, lates take fourteen to fifteen weeks.

Culture
Organic matter is added to pea ground mainly to hold moisture. A dusting of lime before sowing is also beneficial. Plants are better with some support – nets, string or sticks can be used – and taller varieties 3–4ft (90–120cm) need quite substantial support.

Propagation
Seeds of early varieties can be sown under cloches in February and in open ground as soon as conditions allow. Sow maincrops and lates in April/May, and earlies in early June. Sowings after mid-June are liable to be attacked by mildew in late summer and autumn. Sow all seeds 2in (5cm) deep, with the distance between rows equal to the height of the variety.

Harvesting
Pick regularly when pods are young.

Pests and diseases
Mice and birds attack seeds and seedlings. The pea moth lays eggs in the flowers and causes maggots in pods. Spray flowers with derris in the late evening. Fungus diseases attack seeds, so use seed dressings.

Potatoes

Potatoes will grow in most kinds of soil and are often used as the first crop on new ground, with a view to cleaning it of weeds and helping to improve its structure. They are divided mainly into two groups – earlies and lates. Earlies are for digging as soon as the tubers are formed, lates are for leaving to mature in the ground to dig and store for winter use.

Culture
They like slightly acid soil and plenty of organic material immediately round the tubers. Pulling soil up to the stems – earthing-up – is done when the tops are a few inches high, to ensure that tubers are well covered. Exposure to the light turns them green and uneatable.

Propagation
Seed tubers are set 12–15in (30–38cm) apart in rows 20–24in (50–60cm) apart and around 4in (10cm) deep. Time of planting is from mid-March onwards. The tops are at risk from frost until the end of May and should be covered as they come through. April plantings are generally safe.

Harvesting
Dig earlies as required. Lates for storing must mature in the ground. The tops must die down naturally and the skins of the tubers be 'set', ie not easily rubbed off. Store in a dark, frost-proof place.

Pests and diseases
Rough marks on skins are potato scab. Combat by adding organic matter, and avoid liming. Spray fungicide to prevent potato blight, which attacks leaves and stems in July.

Radish

A quick-growing crop that can be used for inter-cropping or as a catch crop, particularly in the spring. Suitable for early sowing under cloches.

Culture
Anything that can be done to ensure quick growth is worth while. A fine tilth, peat or similar worked into the top 2–3in (5–8cm), and water when dry, will help to produce tender crisp roots. Lack of full light encourages leaves at the expense of roots.

Propagation
Sow seeds at intervals from February (under cloches) all through summer if you want them. Broadcast seed in patches or sow in ½in (13mm) deep drills.

Harvesting
Pull when ready.

Pests and diseases
Dust seedling leaves as they come through with derris to deter flea beetle.

Seakale

Grown for its second crops of leaves, which are forced in complete darkness to make them white and crisp.

Culture
One- or two-year-old roots are trimmed of side-shoots, and stood upright in boxes or pots of any kind of compost. They must be kept completely dark, watered and warm, 45–50°F (7–10°C), to force and bleach the new leaves.

Propagation
Can be grown from seeds sown 1in (2.5cm) deep in drills 1ft (30cm) apart, thinning the seedlings to 6in (15cm) apart. Forcing roots take two years to grow from seed, and it is quicker to take pencil-thick pieces of root (called thongs) 6in (15cm) long, and plant with the top inch under the surface in March. These will be ready to dig up and force by October.

Harvesting
Cut when ready.

Pests and diseases
Protect from slugs.

Shallots

One of the easiest vegetables to grow, making a good substitute for onions. Ideal for pickling.

Culture
As for onions.

Propagation
Grown from single bulbs kept from previous year's crop and planted as soon as possible (February/March) 6in (15cm) apart, in rows 12–15in (30–40cm) apart. Bulbs are half-buried in the soil.

Harvesting
Tops start to yellow and drop in July, and by the end of the month they can be dug up and laid out to dry. After a week or so they can be harvested.

Pests and diseases
Trouble-free.

Spinach

There are three main kinds of spinach: summer, winter and spinach beet.

Culture
Will grow in most soils, but tends to go quickly to seed on light ground that dries out. Peat, compost or manure is necessary to hold moisture,

Propagation
Summer spinach is sown in early spring and for succession at two-week intervals. Sow 1in (2–3cm) deep in rows 1ft (30cm) apart, and thin out seedlings to 4–6in (10–15cm). Winter varieties are sown in August. Spinach beet is sometimes known as perpetual spinach and can be sown in April or August.

Harvesting
Leaves must be gathered regularly to ensure new growth.

Pests and diseases
Trouble-free.

Swedes

A vegetable of the turnip family, more popular in the north than the south.

Culture
Needs organic matter in the soil to conserve moisture, and a dressing of lime before seeds are sown if the ground is at all acid.

Propagation
Seeds must not be sown too early—mid-May to early June being about right. Sow 1in (2–3cm) deep in rows 15–18in (38–45cm) apart and thin seedlings to 9–10in (23–25cm).

Harvesting
Swedes are hardy and can be left in the ground to pull whenever needed, or they can be dug up in October and stored in moist sand.

Pests and diseases
Dust seedlings with derris to deter flea beetle. Will contract club root on acid soils.

Swiss chard

A dual-purpose vegetable in which the green part of the leaves is used as spinach, and the white wide mid-rib used as seakale.

Culture
As for spinach.

Propagation
As for spinach.

Harvesting
As for spinach.

Tomato

The best fruits are grown in greenhouses. Outdoor crops are very dependent on the weather.

Culture
'Clean' well-drained soils are essential, as plants are prone to root troubles and soil-borne diseases. Ring culture, soil-less composts and grow-bags are various methods of ensuring a healthy root system. When flowers are open a distribution

of pollen must be ensured by tapping the plants or spraying them with clear water. Flowers drop off if unfertilised or if greenhouse temparatures are too high. Ventilation is essential. Extra feeding of high-potash fertiliser should start when the first fruits are formed.

Propagation
Seed is best sown under glass in pots or boxes. The peat composts are ideal. Where heat is available until end of April, sow in January in 65°F (18°C). For early crops, plants will be ready to set out in March. For planting in cold houses in April, sow seeds in heat in late February. For planting outside, sow in March. Plants must not be put outside until the first week of June, unless protected.

Harvesting
Pick as fruit ripens.

Pests and diseases
Various root rots are caused by infected soils. Botrytis and mildew of fruit and leaves are caused by insufficient ventilation. Outdoor plants will contract potato blight from July onwards. Spray with preventive fungicides.

Turnips

Varieties are available that make small and tender roots quickly. Others can be grown bigger for storing through the winter.

Culture
As for swedes.

Propagation
Sow the early varieties in March and April for succession. Sow maincrop in May, winter varieties in July. Early varieties go 12in (30cm) apart in rows. Thin seedlings to 4in (10cm), lates 18in (45cm) between rows, thin to 9in (23cm). Seeds 1in (2–3cm) deep.

Harvesting
Pull earlies while young and tender. Winter varieties can stand outside, or dig them up and store in sand.

Pests and diseases
As for swedes.

Sowing and Planting Guide

Sow these where they are to grow, and thin out if necessary:

Crop	Sowing time	Distance between rows	Thin out to	Remarks	Use
Beans, Broad	March/April	24in (61cm)	—	Sow 2in (5cm) deep, 4in (10cm) apart. Can also be sown in November	June to August
Beans, French	April/May	18in (45.5cm)	—	Sow 1in (2.5cm) deep, 6in (15cm) apart	July to October
Beans, Runner	May	5ft (1.5m)	—	Sow 2in (5cm) deep, 9in (23cm) apart	July to October
Beetroot	April/May/June	12–15in (30.5–38cm)	6–8in (15–20.5cm)	Can be pulled as soon as big as golf balls or left until autumn and stored in sand	July to March
Beet, Spinach	April/August	15in (38cm)	9in (23cm)	If two or three sowings are made, it is possible to pick all year round	All year round
Beet, Seakale	April/August	18in (45.5cm)	9in (23cm)	Green can be used as spinach, white ribs as seakale	Most of the year
Carrot	March/June	12in (30.5cm)	—	Varieties for pulling young need not be thinned. Main-crop thin to 4in (10cm). Store in sand	All year round
Lettuce	March/August	9–12in (23–30.5cm)	6–12in (15–30.5cm)	Sow every 2–3 weeks for continuous supply. August sowing use winter variety	May to October
Onion (for bulbs)	March and August	12in (30.5cm)	6–9in (15–23cm)	August sowing is of Japanese varieties to stand winter and use in June/July	October to March
Onion (salad)	March/April	10in (25.5cm)	—	Pull and use as needed	June to October
Parsley	March/August	—	4in (10cm)	Takes longer than most things to germinate	June to December
Parsnip	March/April	18in (45.5cm)	6in (15cm)	Can be left in the garden and dug as needed	September to April
Peas	March/June	2ft min (61cm)	—	Space seed out 2in (5cm). Sow two or three times for succession	June to October
Radish	March/August	10in (25.5cm)	—	Sow thinly and often for succession	May to September
Spinach, Summer	March/July	12in (30.5cm)	4in (10cm)	Sow two or three times for succession	May to September
Spinach, Perpetual	March/August	15in (38cm)	6in (15cm)	Leaves can be picked as needed	All year round
Swede	May/June	15in (38cm)	9in (23cm)	Use as needed or can be stored	All year round
Turnip	March/July	12in (30.5cm)	6–8in (15–20.5cm)	Sow two or three times for succession	June to December

Sow these in seedbed and transplant later. Alternatively, plants can be bought at planting out time:

Crop	Sow	Transplant	Distance between rows	Distance between plants	Use
Broccoli, Sprouting	May	July	2ft (61cm)	2ft (61cm)	March to May
Brussels Sprouts	March/April	May/June	2½–3ft (76–91cm)	2½ft (76cm)	September to March
Cabbage, Spring	July/August	September/October	18in (45.5cm)	9–15in (23–38cm)	March to June
Cabbage, Summer	March/April	May/June	18in (45.5cm)	15–18in (38–45.5cm)	July to October
Cabbage, Savoy	March/April	May/June	2ft (61cm)	18in (45.5cm)	September to December
Cabbage (January King)	May	July/August	2ft (61cm)	18in (45.5cm)	November to March
Cauliflower, Summer	March/April	May/June	18in (45.5cm)	18in (45.5cm)	July to October
Cauliflower, Winter	May	July	2ft (61cm)	18in (45.5cm)	March to June
Calabrese	March/April	May/June	2ft (61cm)	18in (45.5cm)	August to October
Kale	May	July	2ft (61cm)	2ft (61cm)	October to April
Leeks	March/April	June/July	18in (45.5cm)	9in (23cm)	November to April

Buy these as plants for setting out at appropriate times:

Crop	Plant out	Distance between rows	Distance between plants	Remarks	Use
Celery (blanched)	June/July	3ft (91cm)	1ft (30.5cm)	Must be earthed up as it grows	October to March
Celery (self-blanching)	June/July	in blocks	10in (25.5cm)	Generally needs water	August to November
Cucumber (outdoor)	June	—	2ft (61cm)	Must be cut when young	July to October
Marrow	June	—	3ft (91cm)	Bush or trailing varieties	August to October
Sweet corn	June	in blocks	12in (30.5cm)	Must have sunny spot	August to September
Tomatoes	June	—	18in (45.5cm)	Straw needed to keep fruit of bush varieties off the ground	August to October
These also have to be bought:					
Onion sets	April	12in (30.5cm)	6in (15cm)	Half bury bulbs when planting	July to March
Potatoes (early and late)	April	24–30in (61–76cm)	10–15in (25.5–38cm)	Earlies can go minimum distance, plant lates at maximum	June onwards
Shallots	February/March	12in (30.5cm)	6in (15cm)	Half bury bulbs when planting	July onwards

January

Maybe it's cold outside! But you'll have to drag on the longjohns and winter woollies and get into the garden. For if you didn't get the job done in the late autumn, this is the best time to prepare the ground for spring sowings.

This means digging, manuring and generally cleaning up the vegetable plot. But don't rush at it as though there's no tomorrow. You'll probably have stuffed yourself silly over Christmas and the New Year, so take it in easy stages and spread the work over three or four weekends. It's an excellent way to work off unwanted weight.

So this is the time to dig the plot and add bulky organic materials such as well-rotted manure, compost or moist peat. It's also the time to decide exactly what vegetables you're going to grow and to work out a rotation plan.

And when you're walking round the veg plot in January, you can tell how good or bad a job you made of vegetable gardening the previous year. For the vegetable garden should *always* be producing – there is no such thing as a fallow period. Even in this bleak month you could be lifting celery, leeks, Jerusalem artichokes and parsnips. All these are crops that can be 'stored' in the soil.

If your veg patch is still providing you with food after Christmas – both fresh and from stores – then it is working well. If not, you might reconsider your sowing and cropping programme.

Jobs for the month

In the greenhouse

Sow, in a temperature of 55–60°F (13–15°C), onions, leeks, cabbage, cauliflower and brussels, all for hardening off and planting outside in March/April.

Sow lettuce for planting into a cold greenhouse or cold frame. Sow tomatoes in 65–70°F (18–21°C) for planting in warm greenhouse in March.

Outside

Manure and dig all vacant ground.

Plan for this year's crops, remembering that 'greens' must be in a fresh place.

Send for seed catalogues and decide which varieties to grow.

Examine all vegetables in store, removing any 'bad' specimens.

Watch for pigeons attacking greenstuff, particularly in bad weather.

Set up early varieties of potatoes in shallow boxes in a light place to chit. Protect from frost.

Protecting winter vegetables

Winter vegetables are among the most valuable crops you can grow because you can harvest them from the garden at a time when fresh produce is at its most expensive in the shops. So it is wise to give these vegetables as much protection as possible from the damaging effects of weather and pests.

1 To prevent wind damage to brassicas, mound up the stems with soil and firm down. In really exposed and windy gardens, brussels sprouts may require individual staking.

2 In rural areas it is also advisable to cover brassicas with netting, as cabbages and the like will be the first choice of any hungry pigeons.

3 Whitefly can be severe during any mild spells in the winter months, so spray with a whitefly killer to keep these horrors at bay. But a word of warning: branded sprays do not kill whitefly eggs, so make several sprayings during the winter.

4 A cloche placed over parsley will ensure a succession of clean, fresh sprigs during the winter, when there is little to pick in the way of herbs.

The difference a greenhouse makes

A greenhouse can be a boon to the gardener because some vegetables can be started up in warmth under glass in January, and by the time the weather's right for seed sowing outside, you will have plants to be setting out – a gain in time of almost a couple of months.

You need a cold frame as well because you can't take plants straight out of the warm and expect them to stand up to whatever March might bring. They go from the greenhouse into the frame, as a halfway house.

So, what with one thing and another, there's a bit of time and trouble involved and, of course, the expense of heating.

If you use heating to the full, however, and raise bedding plants, geraniums, tomatoes and the like, it can be made to pay.

Don't heat a whole greenhouse just to start up a few pots of seeds. There are ways of heating a small area that cost very little.

One of the best and most reliable is the electric soil-warming cable. These cables, well-insulated wires a few feet long, are laid on the greenhouse staging in a bed of sand and plugged into the mains. The pans or boxes of seeds are stood on this, and are quite happy without any other heating in the house whatsoever. If this small area is covered with polythene the effect is of a small greenhouse within a greenhouse.

Paraffin heaters can be arranged to concentrate their heat in a small area, and of course it is possible, however the greenhouse is heated, to enclose a small area of it with polythene to build up a more concentrated 'hot spot'.

The temperature needed to get seeds germinated in January is 55–70°F (13–21°C), the lower figure for such vegetables as lettuce and brassicas, the higher for tomatoes, peppers and cucumbers.

Let's emphasise that with some vegetables there's no advantage at all to be gained from starting them in a greenhouse. There has to be a case made out for doing it.

So here's a list of the things that are worth while sowing now, in January, and why.

Beans, broad

They are one of the first veg that can be sown outside, but if you want to gain a week or two with them sow them 2in (5cm) apart in boxes, or one in a pot, 1in (2–3cm) deep. Put them in the cold frame as soon as they're 1in (2–3cm) high, and plant them out in March.

Brussels sprouts

The earlier they're sown, the bigger the plants grow, and the bigger the plants, the more sprouts they carry. Sow the seeds ½in (13mm) deep in a 5in (12.5cm) pot or pan. Prick them out into a box 2in (5cm) apart, or pot them up separately when they're about 1in (2–3cm) high, and put them in the frame after about two weeks. Plant them out in March.

Cabbage

Treat exactly the same as brussels sprouts for early use. Use a quick-maturing variety such as Hispi or Greyhound.

Cauliflower

As cabbage. Again use early-maturing varieties.

Cucumbers

These are not only started in the warm greenhouse, but are also grown on in the same temperature, so that if you raise them in a small warm spot, they still need the same temperature, 65–75°F (18–24°C) after they are planted out. Sow seeds 1in (2–3cm) deep, singly in 3in (8cm) pots.

Leeks

If you want big leeks, treat as for lettuce.

Lettuce

One of the most useful subjects to sow early. Choose quick-growing varieties such as Fortune or May Queen. Sow ¼in (6mm) deep, prick out 2in (5cm) apart in boxes, harden off in cold frame and plant out in March.

Onions

As for leeks.

Peas

A week or two can be gained by sowing them inside about the end of January. Sow three seeds 1in (2–3cm) deep in a 3in (8cm) pot. Stand in the frame as soon as they are through, and plant them out as they are in groups of three, 4in (10cm) apart in March. Use early varieties.

Tomatoes

These also need warmth to keep them growing as well as for germination. Sow ½in (13mm) deep and keep at a temperature of 65°F (18°C) until they are big enough to pot up separately into 3in (8cm) pots. Keep at not less than 60°F (15°C) and plant in the greenhouse when 6–9in (15–23cm) high.

It is essential for all these early sowings to use a sterilised compost, and best for all seed sowings are the no-soil composts.

Be sure the composts are evenly moist before putting them into pots or boxes. Then water with a fine rose, and allow to drain before sowing seeds.

Cover with glass or plastic and a sheet of paper, but watch carefully and remove the cover at the first sign of seedlings.

Sowing broad beans under cloches

Broad beans can be sown in January, providing they are protected by cloches.

1 Any well dug piece of ground is suitable. Once weather and soil conditions allow, apply a balanced general fertiliser over the whole site.

2 Work in the fertiliser about a week before sowing and rake over the ground to remove large stones; break down large clods of soil and level the site.

3 After breaking down the soil into a workable tilth, cover the sowing site with cloches to help dry out the soil surface and warm the ground.

4 You can sow a double row of beans under cloches. Space seeds 6–9in (15–23cm) apart and 3in (8cm) deep: on heavy ground, dig out the holes with a trowel. Space the rows 9in (23cm) apart.

5 It's always a good idea to sow some extra seeds closer together at the end of the rows to make up for any losses that may occur. Remove the cloches in March or early April.

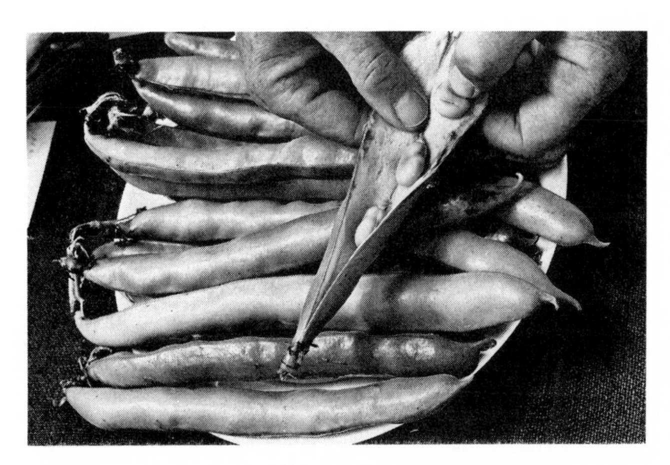

6 And this is what they should look like when they're havested – long pods containing big beans.

Sowing tomatoes

Sow tomato seed in heat for planting in the greenhouse if an early crop is required. For a main crop under glass or for a cold-house planting in spring, delay sowing until February.

1 The drainage holes of plastic seed trays need only a layer of rough peat over them to prevent compost washing out. But some crocks may need to be laid down first in wooden trays with gaps.

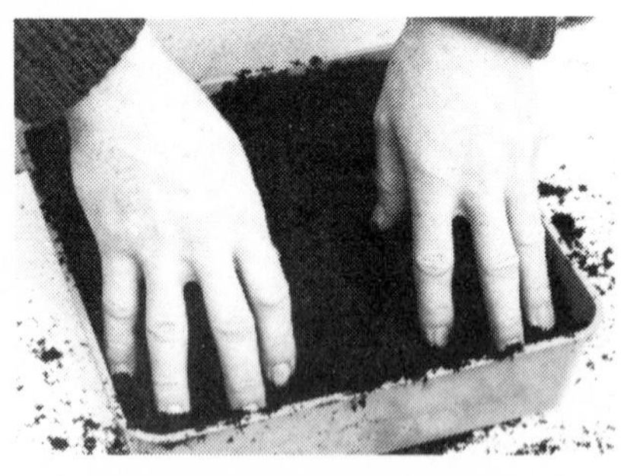

2 Add moist sowing compost and firm down with your fingers, especially in the corners where air spaces can occur. Use John Innes or peat-based compost for tomatoes.

3 A piece of wood is handy for scraping off excess compost, making the level flush with the rim of the tray.

4 A piece of plank fitted with a handle is just right for levelling seed trays. Gently firm the compost down to ½in (13mm) below the rim.

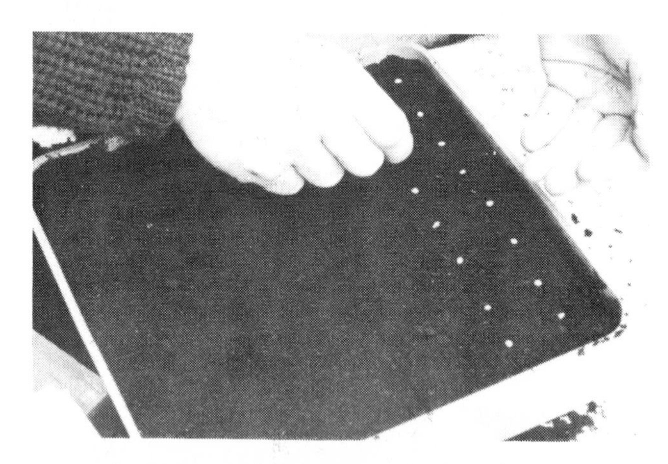

5 Either scatter the seeds thinly and evenly over the compost, or space them out 1in (2–3cm) apart; this will save pricking them out later and disturbing the seedling roots.

6 Using a fine sieve, cover the seeds and use the leveller to firm down the surface very lightly. Place the tray in a heated greenhouse or propagator at 65–70°F (18–21°C).

February

Gardeners hate February. It's the worst month of the winter—wet, cold and windy. The ground may be so hard that it's pointless even considering digging or seed sowing - or so damp that you can't walk on it for fear of half the veg plot's soil sticking to the bottom of your wellies.

And what makes February even more depressing is that every so often an insipid sun will appear and you're deceived into thinking spring has sprung - only to have hopes dashed as the wind gets up again, the heavens open with another deluge of rain; then to cap it all, yet another frost sets in.

If you do get a few days of decent weather during the month, however, there is a lot of useful work you can do.

If you didn't finish it in January, there's still time to dig the plot and add organic materials. But if the weather and the condition of the soil allow you, the most important task is to sow the first of the hardy crops, such as peas, onions, shallots and broad beans.

This means the veg plot is finally underway and the great grow-your-own adventure has started.

Jobs for the month

In the greenhouse

If they were not sown in January, the same seeds can be put in now at same temperatures. Broad beans and peas can also be started at around 45–50°F (7–10°C). Sow beans one in a pot, peas three in a pot. Place in cold frame when 1in (2–3cm) high for planting out in March.

Sow lettuce for planting outside in March and plant early sown lettuce in a cold frame.

Pot up early-sown tomatoes into 3in (8cm) pots, keeping at 60°F (15°C) and in full light.

Ventilate carefully during spells of sunshine.

Outside

Continue all digging.

Sow White Lisbon onions, lettuce, early peas, broad beans and radishes in sheltered places or under cloches. Make small sowings only as others will be put in next month.

Plant Jerusalem artichokes, chives and shallots.

Give spring cabbages a pinch of sulphate of ammonia to each plant, keeping it off the leaves.

Early sowings

The first things that the veg man will be sowing in the open garden are lettuces, radishes and onions, broad beans and peas; and if he is going to grow his own plants from seed, early cabbages, early cauliflowers, brussels sprouts and leeks.

All these should be put in, at the first opportunity, when the ground has dried nicely on top. When this will be depends, of course, on the weather, and to some extent on where you live. It won't be before the middle of February at the earliest, and is more likely to be around the middle to the end of March.

It's safe to say that some will miss the first sowing chance whenever it comes, and for them it may well be the middle of April when they get their first seeds in.

Why, then, talk about it now?

First, because it's absolutely necessary to have the ground ready, and to have the seeds ready at hand to sow without delay when the time comes.

Second, because it's possible to start up the seeds earlier, under cover, in pots or boxes, so that instead of sowing seeds in March, you can be setting out plants. It's possible to gain six weeks in sowing time, and this means three or four weeks at least in cutting time. A very valuable gain indeed when you're looking for early crops.

Does this demand a greenhouse and expensive heating? A greenhouse makes it easier, but for the things mentioned it isn't necessary. They are all quite hardy, and any warmth given them is just to get them germinated a bit more quickly. In fact, if you wait another week or two, say until the middle of February, they can be started in a cold frame or under cloches without any warmth at all. And even this is worth doing, because it all gains time.

Let's talk about sowing them now. In a warm greenhouse be sure to sow lettuce this month – a quick-growing variety such as Fortune, Tom Thumb or May Queen; also early cabbage – Hispi or Greyhound; cauliflowers – one of the Snowball type; and brussels sprouts of any variety. The brussels are sown not to get a particularly early crop, but because sprouts crop better when they have a long growing season.

If you fancy early broad beans or peas, these too can be started, sowing them one bean to a 3in (8cm) pot and three or four peas to a 3in (8cm) pot.

If you have only a cold greenhouse or a cold frame, all these things can be sown inside on a warm windowsill, pricked out or potted on when very small, and put straight into the house or frame. Be ready to cover them with newspaper or sacks over the glass in a frosty spell.

If you have a warm greenhouse start them there, but get them into the cold frame as soon as possible after pricking them out. If they are kept too warm they will grow tall and weak, just the opposite to what is wanted.

The sowing procedure is easy. A moist seed compost is pressed flat into a pot or pan, watered and left to drain, and the seed is sown thinly and covered with around ¼in (6mm) of compost.

For peas and broad beans fill 3in (8cm) pots and press the seeds in about 1in (2–3cm) deep.

These are all quick and easy germinators, and the most important part of the whole business is to be waiting for them coming through – which may be only three or four days – and immediately get them into full light. If they are in a dark place for only a day after germinating, the little seedlings will spoil.

One other warning: don't sow too many of each. Remember, these are only for an early crop, and you'll be growing more of them all later on, sowing them in the open ground. A pinch of seed of each will generally produce thirty or forty plants.

Greens all the year round

It's possible, if you go about it in the right way, to have 'greens' of some kind from your garden every month of the year.

With good planning, a cabbage, a cauliflower, a boiling of brussels sprouts, or broccoli, can be gathered at any time.

Easy enough, of course, in the summer when it takes good planning to ensure that you don't have *too many* cabbages or cauliflowers all at one time, although if you do they can be put into the freezer.

But it's the winter time that tests the programme. Brussels sprouts are the mainstay at that time, of course, but they aren't everything.

The charts below tells the whole story, but there is one important point to emphasise. If you plant 'greens' for all the year round, you must be prepared to grow your own plants from seed.

You have to have the right kinds and the right varieties, and it's no good relying on someone else to supply you with plants. They may not be as concerned as you are to ensure that the variety is right or that they are supplied at just the right time.

You need a bit of warmth for the earliest sowings and a cold frame to harden off plants, but apart from this, all the growing is done outside.

In March you'll need a seed bed, raked down fine for the earliest outdoor sowings, and you'll need another in May.

Spring cabbage seeds go in in August, and you'll want a yard or two for that, but that's all. Sow them all 1in (2–3cm) deep. It's vital to label them correctly because they all look alike when they come up, and if necessary protect them from birds with cotton and from slugs with slug pellets.

Transplant them carefully into their permanent positions when around 6in (15cm) high, firming and watering them in if it is dry.

Sowing times

Early cabbage *Early cauliflower*	Sow in the warm greenhouse in January/February
Summer cabbage *Autumn cabbage* *Summer cauliflower* *Autumn cauliflower* *Early savoys* *Calabrese*	Sow in seed bed outside in March/April
Brussels sprouts	Bigger plants can be obtained by sowing in a warm greenhouse in January/February, but quite satisfactory plants come from outside sowings in March
Winter cauliflowers *Late savoys* *January King cabbage* *Sprouting broccoli*	Sow outside in May
Spring cabbage	Sow outside in August

Harvest your crops at the following times:

January *Brussels sprouts* *'January King' cabbage* *Late savoys*	Brussels are our main winter stand-by. They can be picked over a period of five or six months. Plants are set out in May, June and July—the earlier the better. 'January King' cabbage and late savoys are planted in July/August.
February *Brussels sprouts* *'January King' cabbage* *Late savoys*	'January King' cabbage and late savoys are much alike but have distinctive tastes. Watch for big-hearted specimens bursting towards the end of the month. Use before this happens.
March *Brussels tops and shoots* *Spring 'greens'* *Early purple sprouting broccoli*	Brussels start to shoot this month, but both these and the tops make very good eating. Spring cabbage plants are set out in October. In an early year or where it's been possible to cover with cloches, they can be cut as leaves. Plants of purple sprouting broccoli must be set out not later then the end of July.
April *Spring cabbage* *Purple sprouting broccoli* *Winter cauliflowers*	Spring cabbage will move quickly this month and can be cut and used at all stages of growth. Don't wait for them to heart up. Purple sprouting has to be cut regularly, perhaps twice a week, or it will go to flower and waste. Winter cauliflowers are planted in July.
May *Spring cabbage* *Purple sprouting broccoli* *Winter cauliflower*	Winter cauliflower used to be called heading broccoli. Different varieties heart up at different times in April and June. Two or three varieties are needed if they are wanted throughout the period. They are all planted at the same time in July.

June *Early summer cabbage* *Early summer cauliflower* *Winter cauliflower*	These earliest cabbages and cauliflowers are of quick growing varieties, started in a warm greenhouse and planted out in April. Cloche protection can be given but is not absolutely necessary.
July *Summer cabbage* *Summer cauliflower*	Remember, if you grow these, that peas and beans will be coming into season too. You may not want too many. They are planted in May and June.
August *Summer cabbage* *Summer cauliflower* *Calabrese*	Calabrese is a type of green summer and autumn sprouting broccoli. It grows quickly and continuously throws shoots that have to be cut regularly. Particularly good for freezing. Plants are set out in June and July.
September *Calabrese* *Summer and autumn cabbage* *Summer and autumn cauliflower* *Early savoys*	This can be a glut month if you aren't careful. It's the time when a freezer is very handy. Savoys are planted in June and July. The earliest are sometimes an embarrassment. The biggest and heartiest must be cut, but others will stand until Christmas.
October *Calabrese* *Autumn cauliflower* *Autumn cabbage* *Early savoys* *Early brussels sprouts*	Any cauliflowers heading up may need a leaf or two put across them to protect them from frost. The biggest and best brussels plants may have produced useable sprouts by now, but only pick those that are ready and may deteriorate if not picked and used.
November *Autumn cabbage* *Autumn cauliflower* *Savoys* *Brussels sprouts*	Both the cabbage and cauliflower will be damaged by frost and must be used up this month. Savoys will take over, and more and more brussels will be ready.
December *'January King' cabbage* *Late savoys* *Brussels sprouts*	From now on brussels will need regular picking, always working from the bottom up. 'January King' cabbage and late savoys are unharmed by frost and will stand for several weeks after hearting up.

Artichokes – an alternative to potatoes

In hot, dry and poor soils, Jerusalem artichokes make an excellent alternative to potatoes. They are easy to grow and have the added advantage of being completely hardy during the winter. Artichokes have a distinct, slightly earthy flavour.

1 The tubers are unevenly shaped and bear fairly prominent 'eyes' (buds). Plant only firm, unshrivelled tubers that show no sign of damage.

2 Take out a trench 4-6in (10-15cm) deep in well-dug, well-drained soil in full sun. If more than one row is required, space them out 30in (75cm) apart.

3 Artichokes don't need a rich soil to crop well, but compost or a little rotted manure forked into the bottom of the trench will improve the yield on poor, light soils.

4 Allow 15in (38cm) space between tubers, then fill in the trench and lightly tread down the soil. In exposed, windy gardens, the plants may require staking as the stems gain height.

5 Harvested tubers are best scrubbed clean with a stiff brush when preparing for cooking. They are delicious in their own right as a main vegetable, and they also make an appetising soup.

Lettuce under glass

Lettuce can be sown and grown in the greenhouse during the winter months to give an early salad crop. But lettuce grown in this way are particularly vulnerable to botrytis infection during cold, moist periods, so make sure that condensation does not drip on to the plants at any time. Keep the air moving by ventilating the greenhouse as weather permits.

1 Check lettuce growing under glass for pest and disease damage. Lettuce in pots should be spaced out (so that the plants do not touch each other) to avoid any infections spreading.

2 The lettuce on the right has been infected with botrytis because moisture has dripped on the crown. Get rid of the infected plant immediately, and check that the polythene used as insulation is taut and not causing drips.

3 Keep up a succession of lettuce by sowing a small pinch of seeds in pots.

Radishes

Radishes can be sown from February to the end of May to give a succession of succulent salad crops. If you really have a taste for them, sow at fortnightly intervals.

1 Radishes need a well-drained rich soil and can be sown early in frames or cloches, or on beds previously prepared for later crops, such as runner beans. Rake the soil down into a fine tilth.

2 Sow the seed thinly in drills 1in (2–3cm) deep and spaced 6in (15cm) apart. Pelleted seeds can be spaced ½in (13mm) apart down the rows.

3 Cover the seeds and firm the soil level by tramping down gently. Keep the soil moist and thin the seedlings (from unpelleted seed) to ½in (13mm) spacing when they are large enough to handle.

Talking of radishes, comparatively new on the gardening scene are several varieties of white radishes. Apart from the novel colour, they differ from the common scarlet varieties in that they tend to have a milder flavour. (Picture: Burpee Seeds)

March

At last! The veg plot really starts to come to life in March. The atrocious weather of February is behind us (at least, it should be!) and a warmer sun will start shining for longer periods.

The last of the winter crops, such as celery and brussels sprouts, will be seen off this month – but March also sees the first spring cabbages, sprouting broccoli and cauliflowers. And the light and warmth will put new life into crops that have been dormant through the winter. They will begin to show fresh, green shoots.

But what March really means to the gardener is that now is the time to start sowing in earnest. Except for the tender crops such as marrows, cucumbers, sweet corn and runner beans, virtually every vegetable can be sown outside now. So get weaving!

Weeds, too, will start showing their ugly heads. They will germinate in the increasing warmth, so now's the time to take the winter wraps off the hoe and begin the long, almost perpetual, job of hoeing.

For the good veg plot must be kept free of weeds at all times. You will only get the best out of your vegetable crops by eliminating the competition.

Jobs for the month

In the greenhouse

Peas, beans, onions, leeks, lettuce and all brassicas that were sown in the warm greenhouse should be moved into a cold frame for hardening off. Watch the weather and cover the frame lights with mats or similar at night if very cold.

Sow cucumbers and melons in the greenhouse in a temperature of 65–70°F (18–21°C).

Plant earliest raised tomatoes in permanent positions maintaining them at 60°F (15°C) minimum. Sow tomatoes, aubergines and peppers for planting in cold houses in early May.

Outside

Sow cabbages, cauliflowers, brussels and leeks in ½in (13mm) deep drills for transplanting later.

Sow peas, broad beans, parsnips, carrots, onions, lettuce and parsley where they are to grow. Plant out earlier-sown and well hardened-off lettuce, cabbage, cauliflower, peas and broad beans towards the end of the month.

Plant shallots if not done earlier.

Plant onion sets late in the month.

Set a few early potatoes, although the main plantings will come next month.

Watch for winter cauliflowers heading up and protect curds by laying a leaf or two across.

Transplanting tomatoes

Tomato plants from seeds that were sown early in the new year are just about ready to set out in their growing positions. That is, of course, if they have had the warmth and everything else they've needed all along the line. As most of us know, it doesn't take much to set them on the downward path.

For those of us not lucky enough to have been able to sow tomatoes earlier, the first problems are starting about now. It isn't much trouble to get the seeds germinated as a rule, but the next step, when seedlings have to be moved on from the seed pan or boxes, is critical and it's when many losses occur.

One of the main troubles is that we are often forced to change their environment at this time because they suddenly need more room. This may be from the warmth of a small closed propagator or a warm windowsill in a living room, to the open staging of a greenhouse – and tomatoes don't like sudden changes. The secret, if this new location is forced on you, is not to make the two changes at the same time.

Instead of transplanting and moving them on in one operation, try to spread it a little. Move the seed pan into the new position a day or two before you disturb the seedlings, watering it first so that it won't need any water for as long as possible afterwards.

Do everything you can to even up the conditions. Make sure there are no draughts, and don't put them up near cold glass. A sheet of polythene over them for the first day or so is a good idea, lifting it slightly each day for a week to expose them gradually.

Don't spray water on them, don't use any insecticides in the greenhouse for the time being, and above all don't think that they are going to manage without any warmth at all. They won't. The earliest you can risk standing tomatoes in a cold greenhouse would be at the end of April and even then they should be covered up every night for the first couple of weeks.

Then comes the most dangerous bit – the first transplanting. Well, if the growing conditions are right, there's no doubt that the best time is when the seed leaves have just reached their full size.

But there's no harm in delaying the move if it's not quite as warm as it might be. Every day brings us a bit nearer spring, and you shouldn't move them in a cold spell of weather, especially if they weren't overcrowding each other. Never disturb them when they are dry. The seedlings must be fully charged with water at moving time, so soak the pan from the bottom the day before you intend to make a start.

One of the commonest causes of disaster is using a cold compost. The new stuff must be at least at the same temperature as the pan they are in. This doesn't happen by just standing a bag of John Innes or Levington in a greenhouse for an hour or two. Levington warms up quicker than John Innes, but even this needs a few days. Best plan, if you need to use it quickly, is to spread some out in a shallow layer, being careful not to let it get too dry.

There is in fact a distinct danger in using any compost too wet or too dry. Get it nicely damp, without being sticky, and then warm, and you will have done all you can.

Always pick up the seedlings by the leaves to avoid bruising the stems, and take care also not to crush them when pushing the compost up to them. Set them so that at least half the stem, or a little more, is buried, and finish by spraying them overhead with a fine rose on the can, making sure that the water is not cold. Shade them slightly for a day if the sun is shining, but give them full light for ever after that.

One other thing. Should you prick them off into pots or boxes? It makes no difference at all to their immediate growing on. The benefits of a 3in (8cm) pot are, firstly, that the plants can be moved apart as they grow to give each one more room and light, and secondly that their roots are not disturbed when they are moved to their final positions.

Shallots and onions

Shallots should be set out at the earliest opportunity to give them a long growing season. Root growth, frost and birds will tend to unearth the bulbs, so bury them up to the neck to avoid constant refirming. Onion sets can be planted in the same way.

1 Shallots should be planted in the open as soon as soil conditions allow. Choose plump, firm bulbs that show no signs of disease. Remove withered roots and any loose scales.

2 Birds have the annoying habit of tugging at the withered 'tails' or leaves, so these are best cut off near the neck of the bulbs before planting.

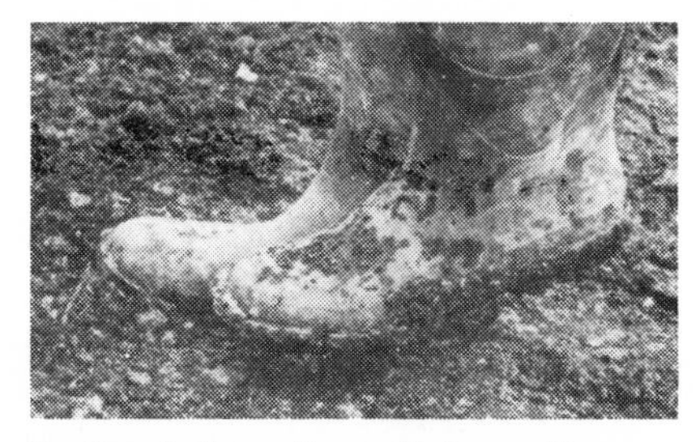

3 Break down the well-dug soil, which has been manured during the winter, apply a balanced general fertiliser and rake level. Firm down the soil by rolling or gently treading the site.

4 Take out shallow drills spaced 12in (30cm) apart and plant the shallots at 6in (15cm) intervals by gently pushing them into the soil.

5 Push the soil up round the bulbs by hand and firm down so that the neck is just protruding. Shallow planting can often lead to the bulbs being lifted out by frost and developing roots.

6 Where birds are troublesome and persist in scratching out the bulbs, cover the rows with strands of cotton or twine. Check periodically for frost lift, and refirm immediately.

Peas

Nothing in the vegetable garden quite compares with the first crop of peas fresh from the pod. Earliest pickings can commence in May, and by sowing successional crops you can be harvesting peas right through to September.

1 After applying a general balanced fertiliser to the soil, break it down into a fine tilth by raking. Use a taut garden line as a guide to making a 6in (15cm) wide drill.

2 Peas are ideally sown 3in (8cm) deep in treble rows within the drill. Space the rows 3in (8cm) apart and the individual seeds 2in (5cm) apart.

3 Cover the seeds by drawing soil into the drill with a hoe.

4 Firm down the soil by lightly treading or by using the head of your rake. If birds are troublesome, cover the drills with netting or cotton to protect the emerging shoots.

5 In colder areas, it is a good idea to cover the rows with cloches to provide better conditions for germination. These will, of course, also keep birds off.

Successful salads

It costs the amateur very little more now to grow salads than it has always done. It's true that seeds, manures, fertilisers and sprays are more expensive, but you have no labour charges to meet, and this is where the commercial growers' costs have risen most.

If you don't count your time, then growing salads, over as long a period as possible, is a cheap way of providing meals for the family.

Don't let anyone kid you that it's easy to produce them all the year round. It isn't. Lettuces, radishes, tomatoes and cucumbers don't grow naturally in the dark months, and it costs more to grow them then than they're worth.

But you can have lettuces and radishes from May to October, and tomatoes and cucumbers from July to October from the open garden. With cloches or a cold frame or greenhouse, you can extend the lettuce and radish season from April to Christmas. With a warm greenhouse, using the heat for only a short time, you can be picking tomatoes and cutting cucumbers from June until November.

Lettuce

Sow May King or Fortune in a warm greenhouse in January for planting into a cold frame or under cloches in March. Sow the same varieties in February in a cold greenhouse for planting outside in April. Sow any summer variety outside in March and on until July at two or three week intervals.

Sow thinly and thin seedlings out to 9in (23cm) apart. Sow a winter variety in August, and protect with cloches in December for cutting in April. To be tender and crisp, lettuce must be grown quickly and this takes a fertile soil with plenty of moisture-holding humus in the top 6in (15cm). To form a heart they must be grown in full, uninterrupted light and have all the room they need to develop.

Cucumber

Cucumbers need a fair bit of warmth, and in the average warm greenhouse are best sown singly in 3in (8cm) pots in March for planting in the greenhouse in April or May. The same varieties – generally known as house or frame cucumbers – can also be sown in the same way in April for planting in a cold frame in June. Outdoor varieties – sometimes known as ridge cucumbers – are sown inside in May for planting outside in June.

All varieties like a rich soil and plenty of moisture. Indoor varieties must be shaded from strong sunshine and need spraying over at least once a day with clear water to create a humid atmosphere. Indoor varieties are not suitable for growing outside, and vice-versa. Plants are always available at garden centres, etc, at the appropriate planting times.

Onion

The variety White Lisbon is the outstanding onion for salads. By sowing a pinch of seed every month or six weeks through March, April, May and June, you can be sure of tender green onions continuously through the summer and autumn. Sow in 1in (2–3cm) deep drills with rows 10in (25cm) apart, and you can start pulling as soon as they are big enough to use. Remember, this is an onion bred exclusively for pulling young. Because of this it can be sown rather more thickly than the varieties you sow to make big bulbs for keeping.

Radish

These can be sown in a cold frame or under cloches in February, outside in March, and on until August at three-week intervals. Only one variety is needed, and Cherry Belle is first class.

Since they grow quickly (in four or five weeks) in rich moist soil, they can be sown as a catch crop on ground set aside for other crops. If sown thinly, no thinning out is needed.

Tomatoes

Seed for the earliest tomatoes is sown in the warm in January, for planting in the warm greenhouse in March. Plants must not be set in a cold greenhouse until late April or early May. Seed for these is sown, still in heat, in March.

Seed for outdoor varieties is sown inside in April, for planting out in early June. Plants can be bought at garden centres, etc, for all purposes, at the proper planting times. It is generally considered that 'bush' varieties are only suitable for growing outside, but apart from this, all varieties can be grown inside or out. Plants outside like warm sheltered positions – against south-facing walls, fences, etc – and where no soil is available, they grow well in grow-bags (polythene bags of complete compost, holding three or four plants). These can also be used in greenhouses where the soil is not suitable.

Pollination of flowers and setting of fruit can be helped by spraying open flowers with a fine spray of water around midday. Feeding with a proprietary tomato fertiliser should be started when the first truss is set and starting to swell. Keep side shoots picked out from 'cordon-grown' plants, and pinch off the tops when six to nine trusses have been made on inside plants, three to five trusses on outside plants. Bush varieties don't need this attention. When the fruit starts to ripen, some of the lower leaves can be taken off to improve air circulation.

Beetroot
These are sown where they are to grow, in 1in (2–3cm) deep drills, and thinned out when small seedlings to 4–9in (10–23cm) apart. They can be pulled as soon as they are big enough to use, and others can be left to be lifted in the autumn and stored in sand through the winter.

Cabbage
Some varieties, Winter Salad and Winter White make hard, tight heads that can be cut in the autumn to be stored in a cool, dry place during the winter and used as needed. They are eaten raw, shredded like lettuce. Sow in a seed bed in May and transplant when 6in (15cm) high, 18in (45cm) apart all ways.

Carrots
Young shredded carrots are an attractive addition to salads. Sow outside in April, May and June, ½in (13mm) deep, and pull as needed. They can be sown under cloches or in a cold frame in February and March for earlier pulling. Early Nantes is a suitable variety.

Chicory
Sow seeds of Witloof variety in May or June, outside in 1in (2–3cm) deep drills. Thin the seedlings to 9in (23cm) apart. Lift the roots in autumn, and store in sand to use as needed. They must be forced in complete darkness to produce the white conical heads known as chicons.

Plant several roots in a 9in (23cm) pot up to their crowns in any kind of soil, water and cover with another pot or a black polythene bag. They will grow in cold conditions, but are much quicker in heat. The roots are thrown away after forcing.

Chives
These are an easy-growing perennial of the onion family. The green leaves can be cut at any time, and chopped or snipped to take the place of salad onions. A few bulbs planted almost anywhere will soon spread into a useful clump.

Mustard and Cress
Can be sown and grown under cover at any time of the year. Sow seeds thickly on the surface of any layer of compost or fine soil, and keep moist. Cut with sharp scissors when 2–3in (5–8cm) high. To cut at the same time, sow cress four days before mustard. Land cress is similar to water cress. Sow seeds outside at any time from May until August and cut the leaves as needed.

Sowing parsnips

Parsnips like a deep, friable soil.

1 Choose a piece of ground that has been deeply dug, but not recently manured. Break down the soil and rake level after applying a general fertiliser.

2 Short- and intermediate-rooted varieties can be sown in drills 1in (2–3cm) deep.

3 Long-rooted parsnips should be sown in pockets of rich compost. A crowbar is the ideal tool for making deep, tapering holes at 9in (23cm) intervals.

4 Sow three to four seeds in the compost pockets, or as groups spaced 9in (23cm) apart in the drills. The groups can be thinned out later to leave the strongest seedlings.

Take a tip . . .

- Radishes don't make good roots if they are too close together. Pull a few seedlings out when they are very small . . . this is especially important where it is obvious they have been sown too thickly.

- Shallots should have really taken hold by the end of March, but a look along the rows may find one or two that are partly out of the ground. One more push in should be enough.

- Kohl rabi has a cabbage-cum-turnip flavour that may be liked as a change. It can be sown from March until the end of June, thinned out when big enough, and is ready to eat in 12 weeks.

- Celery seed goes in at any time in the next week or two. It needs warmth in the greenhouse, and it will need pricking off into boxes a bit deeper than the ordinary seed box. Tomato trays are about right. The white varieties are best for eating before Christmas; the pink varieties are hardier and best for using later. Both types need wrapping or earthing-up to get them blanched. 'Self-Blanching' and 'American Green' both blanch without being covered, but are best planted 9in (23cm) apart in blocks, rather than in rows.

A traditional way of blanching celery . . . encasing the stems in pipes.

April

Dodgy! That's the word to describe April. Though the days are starting to get much longer, the weather can change dramatically in the time it takes you to say 'Spring's arrived!' Sunshine and warmth can turn in an instant to cold winds and pouring rain, and there's still the danger of frosts.

Potatoes are particularly vulnerable to hard frosts, so earth-up the foliage as soon as it appears to provide them with some protection.

If the weather permits (and in an average year it will), continue sowing peas and salad crops for succession, and make sowings of all other vegetables if you didn't get the job done last month. But remember, it's still too early to sow or plant out tender vegetables such as marrows, cucumbers and runner beans.

You should still be cropping from the veg plot in April. There should still be some leeks around, and the spring cabbage will be at its very best. A word of warning here: don't leave spring cabbages in the ground too long as they soon grow tough and coarse.

Jobs for the month

In the greenhouse

Tomatoes can be planted in cold greenhouses at the end of the month, but cover them with newspaper on cold nights. Earlier-planted tomatoes will need supports and attention to side-shooting.

Sow seeds of outdoor tomatoes around the middle of the month.

At the end of the month, sow marrows and outdoor cucumbers (one seed in a 3in (8cm) pot), French beans and runner beans, all for planting out at the end of May or early June.

Ventilate more as weather improves.

Prop up frame lights over lettuce around the middle of the day.

Sow celery seeds and sweet corn, the latter in a pot.

Outside

Sow peas, radishes and lettuce for succession, also carrots, beetroot, summer spinach, kohl rabi, celeriac and chicory.

Plant asparagus and globe artichokes.

Plant all potatoes this month, and earth-up any planted earlier and showing through to protect them from frost.

Run a Dutch hoe alongside rows of seedlings as soon as they can be seen.

Watch for onion sets and shallots lifting out of the ground. Re-firm in.

Prepare sites with manure for marrows and outdoor cucumbers.

Potatoes

Potatoes will grow, after a fashion, almost anywhere. This doesn't mean however that they are bound to produce a crop. In fact it's possible, as a lot of people who planted them in a drought year found out, to dig up fewer tubers than you put in. You can have tops with no bottoms at all.

But give them everything they need and they are the most productive of all our veg. They need a combination of the following conditions:

Healthy seed to begin with

Plenty of food and drink, because they are a hungry crop

Ground free from pests and disease, and measures taken to keep these troubles away

Good all-round uninterrupted light, because

good light affects the production of tubers

And last but not least, time: they can only get to maximum size in a full growing season.

Let's take a look at each of these things.

Seed

Like everything else that is propagated vegatatively, a diseased plant produces diseased offspring. The trouble is that the most insidious and destroying disease of potatoes – potato virus – doesn't show in the tubers. It is only by close inspection of the parent plants that it can be detected.

This is why it is always preferable to buy only stock that has been certified, which means that the growing plants were inspected and certified as clean last season.

Good crops can be grown from other tubers, but there is always a risk of virus considerably lessening the weight.

Scab is the most common disease. It is often found on seed certified as virus-free. But it does not affect the weight of the crop and, in any case, it is only skin-deep, and peels off without damaging the tuber.

Soil

There is no doubt that there is an ideal potato soil, a type that occurs naturally in some districts and is almost impossible to reproduce in others. The big potato-growing areas often have a fine silty soil, easily worked, well charged with a naturally occurring humus, and, although fairly light and drying on the surface, well supplied from underneath with water.

Most gardens can, however, be made better for potatoes than they are. Well-worked soil, which has been dug during the autumn and winter and which has humus dug in and spread on the top after digging, is better than spring-dug lumpy ground. More humus – peat, leafmould, old manure, etc – placed round and in contact with the tuber at planting time also helps. A balanced fertiliser, Growmore or similar, should be sprinkled in the hole or trench and more given as soon as the rows can be distinguished above ground, to ensure that the essential nutrients are available.

If you want to go further still – and potatoes will stand it – they react very well to foliar feeding (feeding through the leaves). An overhead spraying with any recognised foliar fertiliser, once or twice about half way through the season, will add valuable weight.

Pests

Few pests worry the growth of potatoes. If the microscopic and unseen potato eelworm infests the ground, you should not be planting it with potatoes anyway. But apart from this, the worst pest is undoubtedly slugs.

Even these don't stop the plants growing, though of course they can ruin the tubers. If you have any soot, scatter it in at planting time as a deterrent, but slug pellets along the rows are the only real killers; even they are not wholly successful in bad attacks.

Some years cutworms can be a nuisance. These are soil caterpillars that attack the tubers. They are controlled with a soil insecticide sprinkled round each plant as it comes through the soil.

Planting distance and light

A single row of potatoes across a garden will quite easily produce a crop three times the weight of that coming from a row surrounded on all sides by other rows. This is, of course, partly because there is not so much competition for food, but it is mainly because the leaves receive more uninterrupted light from all sides.

If you can set potato rows a couple of yards apart, with a smaller or later-planted crop between, it pays handsomely. If they have to be in a patch, don't overcrowd them, particularly the lates. A foot between sets and 24in (60cm) between rows is the minimum, with 18in (45cm) and 30in (75cm) even better.

For earlies, 12in (30cm) and 20in (50cm) is enough. If you do plant in single rows, earlies and lates need go only 10in (25cm) apart.

Time

Finally, for maximum crop, every day of growing time is important. Earlies should be dug only as needed, because they are continually putting on weight while the tops are green. Lates are losing growing time every minute they are out of the ground. Don't hesitate to plant after the middle of April.

Planting potatoes

Provided that the ground is workable, April is the month to plant maincrop potatoes. These are heavy feeders, so dig plenty of organic material (compost or manure) into the base of the planting drills, and then apply fertiliser as you fill in.

1 Add an organic fertiliser, such as well-rotted manure, or a proprietary fertiliser to the drills.

2 Seed tubers should ideally have a cluster of ½-1in (13mm-3cm) shoots at planting time.

3 Plant the tubers 5in (12cm) deep, preferably in a 'nest' of peat or leafmould. In limey soils, this will help deter scab disease.

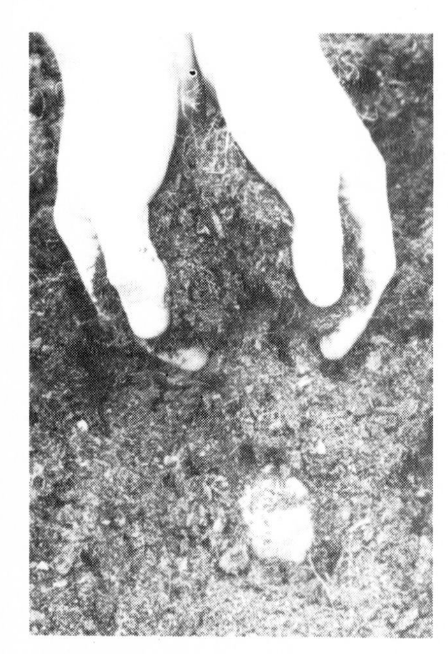

4 Space maincrop varieties 15in (38cm) apart in the rows, allowing 24-30in (60-75cm) between the rows. Cover the tubers with some more peat or leafmould.

5 Fill in the trench or drill so that the soil is slightly mounded over the row, and then add a balanced fertiliser at 4oz per square yard (120gm per square metre). A similar feed should be given when the shoots appear.

6 After planting, gently fork along each side of the rows to remove footmarks and keep the soil open.

Tomatoes

Funny things, tomatoes. In one sense it can be said that they are more particular about the soil they are in than almost anything else we grow. Yet in another sense they aren't too fussy about soil at all.

It seems a contradiction, but the truth is that we are talking about two different things. They are definitely fussy about the soil being clean and fresh, because they are prone to attack from soilborne diseases. They do not mind so much about the type of soil, whether it be heavy or light, even rich or poor; if it is poor, tomatoes take kindly to being fed during their growth anyway.

These two facts account in the main for what so often happens when a new greenhouse is put up and tomatoes are set in the existing borders for the first time. Almost invariably they do well. The ground is free of tomato-destroying diseases, because it may well have never seen tomatoes before, and with quite ordinary watering and feeding, a good crop is gathered.

Almost invariably too, the plants and the crop deteriorate in subsequent years. The borders become infected, and then, whatever is done in the way of care, watering and feeding, it is all for nothing. Plants collapse and die.

The betting is then, that if you have a new greenhouse, your borders, with quite ordinary preparation, will produce a worthwhile crop. They may well do it a second year, but after that beware, you may be backing a loser.

There are, then, various ways of remedying this. You can sterilise the soil, and there are several ways of doing it, chemically or otherwise, none of which is easy or convenient.

You can change all the soil, again not convenient for most of us. You can plant into grow-bags, sealed polythene bags of complete growing compost, which contain the roots completely so that they do not come into contact with the infected soil.

You can dig out the soil and replace it with gravel or ashes for growing by the ring-culture method. Or, something akin to that, you can cover the soil with a sheet of polythene and put on it a layer of peat or straw, again for setting 'rings' on. Or you can grow in bales of straw, by making a hole in each one and planting into just enough soil to get the tomato started, its roots then spreading into the straw itself.

The object of all these operations, is to insert the plants into a new, fresh, growing medium. And because tomatoes aren't too fussy about the type of soil they are in, they will grow well in any of the ways.

Once you have the method of growing settled, and with all precautions taken regarding clean soil, the time of planting and the type of plant are critical.

In a heated greenhouse, time doesn't matter so much, but in a cold house it can be fatal to plant too soon. One cold night can check them so badly that they may never fully recover. The end of April is taking a chance, the middle of May is better. That fortnight, apparently lost, can easily be regained by the plants getting quickly away.

Planting outside, of course, must be delayed even further. The end of May is about as early as they can be risked, and even then some covering may be necessary at night.

For cold-house or outside planting, plants must have been well hardened-off. Those that have come straight from a warm greenhouse will suffer whatever the weather is or does. They go a steely blue colour, which is a sure sign of a check from cold, and almost invariably the seed leaves drop off.

Incidentally, when buying plants, always look for these seed leaves. If they are missing, you know that at some time all was not well with the plants.

Plants are at their best size for setting out where the first truss is just showing as minute green buds in the growing tip. In general it is best to buy plants in pots rather than from boxes. Always set plants about 1in (2–3cm) deeper in the compost than they are, and always water in.

One last essential for planting into a greenhouse border. The ground must be well soaked with water beforehand. Flood it thoroughly, and test with a trowel to see it has gone well down. A dry sub-soil is the cause of many of the tomato failures with plants under cover.

Runner beans

In milder districts, runner beans can be sown outdoors in the middle of April. But they will need the protection of cloches early on just in case there are snap frosts as the shoots emerge.

1 Runner beans can be sown where the ground has been warmed up under cloches. The condensation on this polythene tunnel cloche is a sign of warmer conditions under the cloche.

2 Sow the seeds 3in (8cm) deep in double rows spaced 12in (30cm) apart. Allow 6in (15cm) between each seed in the rows. Replace the cloche to provide protection from frosts.

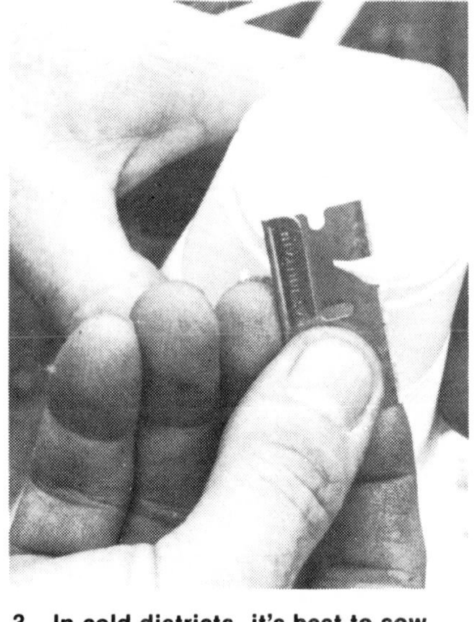

3 In cold districts, it's best to sow the beans under glass. Individual seeds can be sown in small pots, and used plastic cups are ideal once drainage holes have been made.

4 Use a rich well-drained compost and drop the seeds, eye upwards, into holes made 1–1½in (2–4cm) deep. Germinate in a temperature of about 50–55°F (10–13°C).

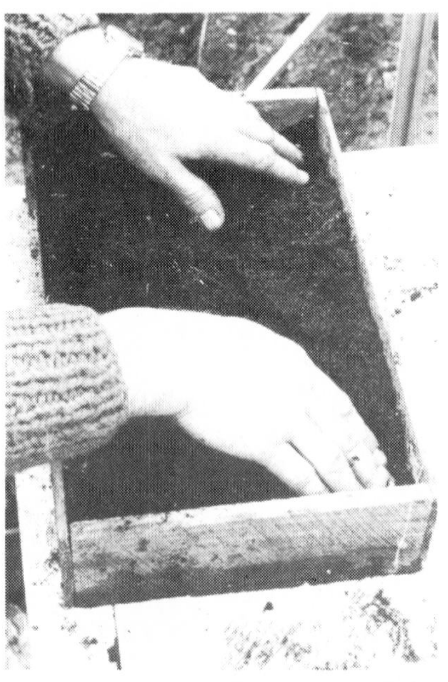

5 Larger batches can be raised under glass in seed boxes filled with compost. Moisten and gently firm down, particularly in the corners of the container.

6 Between fifteen and twenty beans can be raised in a standard seed box. Later, as the plants grow away, apply a liquid feed each week.

Asparagus

It's well worth trying delicious asparagus in the permanent part of your vegetable plot. This vegetable is not difficult to grow provided the site is well drained. Don't start to cut the emerging stems too early: allow at least two years' growth before harvesting one-year crowns, or one year's growth for two-year crowns.

1 Take out a trench 12in (30cm) wide and 9in (23cm) deep on ground well dug and manured during the winter. Make sure that all perennial weeds are removed.

2 Asparagus plants prefer a light soil, but on heavy soil make sure the site is well drained. Mound up the soil to form a ridge along the middle of the trench.

3 Try to plant the crowns as soon as you get them to prevent the roots from shrivelling. Spread the roots evenly over the ridge in the trench.

4 Crowns are spaced 9in (23cm) apart in the trench. If more than one row is required, allow 36in (90cm) between them. After spacing, cover the crowns with 3in (8cm) of soil.

5 Gently firm down the soil and fill in the rest of the trench. Keep the rows hoed to keep the weeds down, and you can start cutting in the second year after planting one-year crowns.

May

Careful! The weather should be really good by now and, to all intents and purposes, summer has arrived. But there is still the danger of hard, snap frosts – and experience will show you that the threat of frosts hangs around until the end of the month.

So don't be caught out by assuming that you can sow or plant out tender vegetables, simply because the month gets off to a warm start. One night of frost later on could decimate your entire crop of marrows, cucumbers, sweet corn and runner beans.

Play it safe, then. Do not sow these until the third week of May and, if you have plants, delay setting them out until the beginning of June.

Some crops, especially fast-growing varieties, will need watering this month. Never let the soil dry out. But don't water in strong sunshine – do it in the cool of the morning or evening so that the vegetables get the maximum benefit of the welcome soakings.

Weeds will continue to appear as fast as you can hoe them, but it's important to get them out as soon as they show. There's nothing more laborious than trying to clear a veg patch infested with weeds. And, of course, if you allow them to grow unchecked, they will eventually throttle the veg crops.

The first pests will fly in in May, blackfly in particular. Be ready for them.

Jobs for the month

In the greenhouse

Runner and French beans, marrows and outdoor cucumbers can be given a slightly earlier start by sowing in a cold house or cold frame at the beginning of the month. Sow one seed in a 3in (8cm) pot, for planting out in early June.

Plant all tomatoes, aubergines and peppers under glass by the end of the month.

Spray flowers of early-planted tomatoes with clear water around midday to help setting. Feed when first fruits are about marble size.

Plant cucumbers in a cold house or cold frame towards the end of the month.

Prick out celery and harden off in a cold frame.

Outside

Plant out all cabbages, brussels, cauliflowers, etc, when 4–6in (10–15cm) high. Firm well and water in if dry.

Sow seeds of winter cauliflowers, winter cabbage and sprouting broccoli after the middle of the month.

Sow more salads and peas for succession.

Sow runner and French beans in permanent positions, also marrows, sweet corn and outdoor cucumbers. Guard against slugs with slug pellets.

At the end of the month, plant well-hardened tomatoes. Be prepared to cover at night in case of frost.

Thin out earlier sowings of carrots, beetroot, onions and lettuce. Of these, only lettuce transplant successfully.

Tender veg

Some of the vegetables we grow have to do everything they are going to between frosts. As that is the short period between the end of May and some time in September – three months or so – it can be seen that neither we nor they have to waste any time.

We can, in fact, give them valuable extra weeks by sowing the seeds and getting them started up under cover so that by the beginning of June we have plants to set out, instead of seeds.

For the slower-growing of this group of frost-vulnerable veg – tomatoes, peppers and aubergines – this earlier inside start is absolutely essential. Without it they would never have time to bear and ripen a reasonable crop. Seeds of marrows, cucumbers, sweetcorn and runner beans can be sown outside and very good crops grown. But an inside start, even for these, gains valuable time and is always worth doing. It not only means that the crop will be ready slightly earlier but also, because the plant has a longer time to grow, the crop may be heavier too.

Let's get the date settled for setting out started plants, whichever they are – or as near settled as we can. It will be slightly different according to the area. The north and all exposed places will be ten days or so later than the south and sheltered spots. If we take May 25 as about average, the date of the last frost might be a week or so either way, and everyone must weigh up the chances in his own particular district and garden. If protection can be given with glass or polythene at night, mid-May can be planting date anywhere, but there must be no forgetting the covering job, nor indeed the uncovering job next morning.

Watch the weather forecasts closely and take no chances.

Sowing inside

The date for sowing seeds inside to give us these early plants has to be watched carefully too. If put in too soon, the plants will be ready to go out before our safe planting date has arrived. It only takes a few days' delay for them to get too big or pot-bound.

Runner beans, for instance, will start to climb and twist round themselves and each other, and get into an unholy tangle. Far better to have just two nicely opened leaves and a small growing point.

The last week in April or the first week in May is just right for sowing beans, marrows, cucumbers and sweet corn in a greenhouse or cold frame, or even indoors. They can go in boxes 2–3in (5–8cm) apart or in individual pots. Pots are better for transplanting from, and almost any compost will do. It is not too late either to sow tomatoes, peppers and aubergines, although plenty late enough, and really you should aim to have plants of these 2in (5cm) or so high by now.

Sowing outside

As already said, only quicker-growing subjects can be sown outside in the places where they are to grow. They take only a week or so to come through and be vulnerable to frost, and the third week in May is therefore the best all-round sowing time, unless a cloche or something similar can be put over for protection.

The runner-bean trench should have been prepared earlier, the supports should be in place and everything ready for sowing one bean to a stick or string. Sow a few extra at the end of the row in case spares are needed.

Individual sites for marrows and cucumbers can be prepared now. Dig out the top spit of soil 1 yard (or 1 metre) square, turn manure, compost or something similar into the next spit down, and replace the top soil, mixing it with some peat and a sprinkling of fertiliser such as Growmore. Mark the spot with a stick in the centre and leave to settle.

Much the same preparations can be made for tomatoes, aubergines and peppers, remembering that they particularly like warm sunny spots protected from the wind. Often a suitable place can be found on a patio or against a wall or fence where there is no soil at all, and it is in such places that the modern gro-bag method of planting comes into its own.

Taking care with outdoor tomatoes

Poor tomatoes sometimes recover enough to give you a fair crop, but you have a far better chance if you start with good plants – particularly if they are to grow outside. They don't have much time anyway and time lost in recovering from a check can never be regained. The crop weight is bound to be affected.

Similarly, plants that are late and small will give a lesser crop, simply because of the time factor.

In most districts the end of May is the time to be planting tomatoes outside, covering them up at night if a frost is forecast and, of course, always protecting them from possible cold winds in some way.

But be sure that your plants are good enough to give you a fair chance. If they're too old, they will have been harmed by pot-bound roots or, if in shallow boxes, the plants will have been drawn up, thin and weak. They will also be hard and tough in the stem, the first truss will be in flower or possibly carrying small fruits, and they will almost certainly be starved and a poor colour.

One or all of these things will delay new growth, and will be bound to mean less fruit in the end.

It is better to have plants that are too young, but even these have to spend time catching up, and it can easily mean one truss less than from plants at just the right stage.

What then, is this right stage? It is generally considered that plants are right for transferring to their permanent positions when the first truss can just be seen in the growing tip – not the open flowers, and certainly not the fruit; just the green unopened buds.

Plants should be short and stocky (although this differs slightly with different varieties) a dark green – but not a bluey-green – and with their seed leaves still on. The seed leaves are the first pair of leaves the plant made, low down on the stems.

The trouble is that plants don't remain at this desirable stage for long. If you're buying them, it's worth looking around a bit to find some, but if you grow your own from seed, it's worth going to no end of trouble to produce plants that will be just right for outside planting at exactly the right time.

It's best to keep your own records of sowing and planting-out dates, and if you're wrong one year, adjust it the next to get it right. Most people sow too soon. Around the first week in April seems to be about right, but it is best to find out for yourself.

The site for outdoor tomatoes is more important than the soil. The plants will grow almost anywhere, even in windy, exposed places. But to get the maximum crop of ripe fruit, choose, if you can, a south-facing wall or fence, on which the sun shines directly all day, and which will hold some of the day's warmth and give it back at night.

If the wind is persistent from either side, some kind of barrier will make all the difference.

Chopped-up turves, leafmould, old manure, grit and a dressing of Growmore will make a good growing medium, either to replace the existing soil and worked into it, or to fill a container of some kind.

And speaking of containers, the most difficult way to grow tomatoes is to pot them up into clay pots, and stand them completely exposed on some concrete or paved yard. It is almost impossible under these conditions to keep them watered and fed correctly, unless they receive almost undivided attention.

Bottomless whalehide pots standing on boxes, ashes or peat to give a kind of ring culture make it easier.

Little can go wrong with the actual planting. Pinch off the bottom couple of leaves and set the plants about 1in (2–3cm) deeper than their present soil line. Firm them with the fingers and above all water them in individually.

It is quite possible for the root-ball of compost from a pot to dry out even if the surrounding soil is quite damp.

Don't let them waste any time. Even an hour or two of standing still will mean a tomato or two less from the total crop.

Time for a hoe-down

A Dutch hoe is the veg gardener's best friend at this time of year. A few minutes spent with it regularly when the sun is shining will save a lot of toil, tears and sweat, not only a bit later on in the season but also in years to come. If a weed goes to seed its progeny will be around for a long time – 'One year's seeds, seven years' weeds.'

A word about the persistence of weed seeds might not be out of place here, because a lot of newcomers to the game often wonder where they keep coming from.

By their very nature they are survivors. They are weeds because they are able to carry on where other things die, and one of their qualities, if we can call it that, is the ability of their seeds to stay alive for a long time, even if they are in a hopeless position to grow.

This means that if, say, they are buried in manure or compost, they can be dormant for many years, springing into life only when conditions are right.

It also means that if they are not near enough to the surface of the soil in the garden, they don't germinate, but lie dormant, waiting quite comfortably.

When a weed goes to seed as a rule it scatters its large family far and wide by various means. And though it's possible for some of them to germinate in the same year, many get turned in and buried when the digging is done.

Whether they appear the next season or not depends on the depth they are in the soil. Those in the top 2in (5cm) will almost certainly germinate and grow the following spring, but those below will bide their time, possibly for years, until they too get near enough to the soil surface. Digging and soil disturbance in subsequent years does just this.

However careful and conscientious we are, weeds are a part of gardening from which we cannot escape. They blow in from surrounding patches, and are also brought in with manure; but most often they come from plants that seed in the same garden.

The trouble is that many weeds make seeds very early in their lives. The speedwell, for instance, is carrying its pretty blue flowers when only a week or two old. So are chickweed and groundsel, and groundsel can even go on producing flowers and seed when laid on top of the ground after hoeing.

Dutch hoeing works in two ways. If properly done, it leaves seedlings on top of the ground with roots exposed to the sun and wind, and when they are very small, even weeds cannot survive this for long.

It also works by depriving perennial weeds of their leaves, and however persistent they are through their underground spreading roots, no weed can live for ever without making leaves.

The technique, however, must be to hoe the ground before the leaves show. If they are left to make leaves, no matter how persistently you have kept them hoed off before, they will recover and you are back almost to square one again.

The counsel of perfection then, is to hoe regularly when the surface is dry, whether there are any weeds showing or not.

The essence of the Dutch hoe is that it is used working backwards. That gives you the advantage of not having to tread on ground you have hoed, thus leaving no footmarks and, more important, avoiding treading hoed-off weeds back into the surface, where they may well re-root and recover.

It is important not to dig in too deep with the blade. It should be at such an angle that when held in a comfortable working position, it slides horizontally just underneath the surface.

The blade should, of course, be kept sharp and clean, and the hoeing should be done systematically so that patch is hoed all over and nothing is missed.

Dwarf beans

Dwarf beans need a warm soil, and sowing in cold ground may result in the seeds rotting. So in chilly districts it pays to cloche the ground a week or so before sowing, to warm up the soil. And after sowing, keep the cloches on until the plants are showing.

1 Ideally, dwarf beans are sown on ground manured during the previous winter. Apply a balanced fertiliser, raking the soil down into a fine tilth a day or so before sowing.

2 Take out drills 2in (5cm) deep, using a garden line to get straight rows. If more than one row is needed, allow 18in (45cm) between them.

3 If the soil is dry, water the drill before sowing the seeds at 6in (15cm) intervals. Sow some extra seeds closer together at the end of the row to make up for any 'misses' later.

4 Cover the seeds with soil and firm down with the back of a rake or, on light soils, gently tread firm. And remember, covering the row with cloches will provide warmer conditions in cold districts.

Sweet corn

Sweet corn is best started in the greenhouse, but you can also obtain a good crop by sowing outside in May.

1 After applying a dressing of general fertiliser, rake over the sowing site. Sweet corn likes a sunny, sheltered position to give good results.

2 All sweet corn should be 'block' sown or planted as it is wind-pollinated. Draw out short drills about 1in (2–3cm) deep and spaced 18–24in (45–60cm) apart.

3 Sow the seeds in pairs at 15–18in (38–45cm) intervals down the drills. Later, the weaker seedling of each pair should be removed. Sow a few extra seeds at the end of each row to make up for any 'misses'.

4 Cover the seeds by drawing soil in from the sides of the drills, and gently firm by tamping down with a rake-head. Water the site well if it is dry.

Sweet corn is a valuable crop to grow – not only because it tastes good, but it also freezes well, so can be eaten all the year round. It has to be harvested at exactly the right time, but there is a simple way of checking whether cobs are ready to pick: press one of the seed grains with your thumb nail and if the liquid that flows out looks like water, the corn has yet to mature . . . if it is the colour of milk, the cob is ready for harvesting.

Tomatoes in an unheated greenhouse

Tomato plants can now be planted in an unheated greenhouse into the bed soil (provided the soil has been sterilised), growing bags or rings. The latter two methods are best, especially if your tomato crop has been affected by soil pests or disease in past seasons. Whalehide rings can be bought, but you can also make your own from felt or even linoleum.

1 When growing in rings, put down a layer of heavy-gauge polythene sheeting to isolate the aggregate (on which the pots will stand) from the soil.

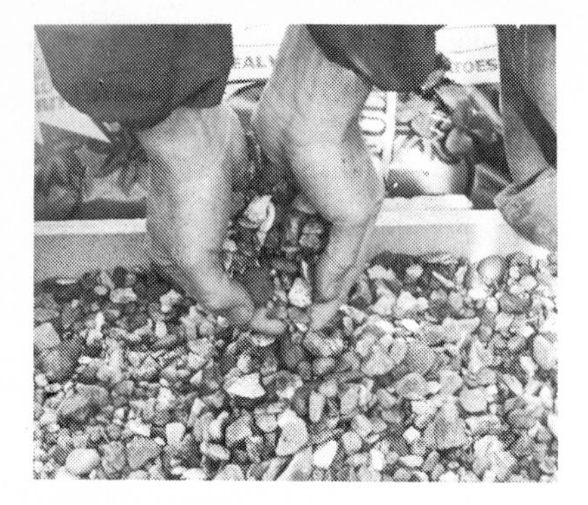

2 Make some slits through the polythene to provide drainage, then fill in a trench or trough with an aggregate such as granite chips, coarse sand or gravel to a depth of about 6in (15cm).

3 Rings measuring 9in (23cm) wide are spaced 20–24in (50–60cm) apart on the aggregate and filled to within 2in (5cm) of the top with a peat-based compost.

4 Allow the aggregate and the compost to warm up for a day or two before planting the tomatoes. Insert cane supports as you plant to avoid damaging roots later.

5 During the early stages of growth, all watering should be done into the rings; this also applies to any feeding necessary. As the first flowers open, the aggregate itself can be damped down.

Planting brussels sprouts

Brussels sprouts need a firm site if they are to 'button up' and give a good crop. If you are pulling transplants from a seed bed, water well the night before lifting. Plants from trays are best planted with a trowel, but firm in well.

1 Apply a dressing of general fertiliser to the ground and rake in well. Tread the site firm and make shallow drills with a hoe or inverted rake-head, spacing them about 30in (75cm) apart.

2 To help prevent attacks of club root and root fly, it pays to make up a slurry of calomel dust and water.

3 Dip the transplants in the slurry, making sure that the whole root system is covered for maximum protection.

4 Use a dibber or trowel to plant the brussels sprouts, spacing them 30in (75cm) apart in the rows. Firm in well.

5 Water the transplants in and keep them moist in dry spells so that they establish themselves quickly. To discourage bird damage, it is wise to erect simple scarers.

June

During June and July, the veg plot should look its best. With winter truly behind us, lots of crops should be maturing fast and showing lush green growth. This is when you really start seeing the fruits of your hard labour.

You should be able to harvest salad crops – lettuces, spring onions, radishes and the like – every day. The tender young broad beans should be ready for picking, and the root crops, potatoes included, will form rows of abundant foliage, promising great crops to come.

But don't be lulled into a false sense of security. The veg plot looks good and it'll stay good – but only if you continue to work on it.

Keep hoeing those weeds out (remember, they can go on the compost heap, so they are of some use) and watch out for pests. They come into their own in June, so a daily check of all your crops is advisable. If you spot any, take action immediately.

June also heralds those long, hot, balmy days of summer – and that means your crops will need gallons of water. Yes, they do need *gallons*. A common mistake made by many new vegetable gardeners is not to give their crops enough water. They waltz around the plot with a couple of cans of water thinking a sprinkle here and a sprinkle there is sufficient.

All they're doing, in fact, is to moisten the surface of the soil, leaving the roots absolutely parched. The only way to water the vegetable garden thoroughly is to use a garden sprinkler, leaving it on for a couple of hours or so at a time during really dry spells. And remember, do your watering early in the morning or in the evening.

Jobs for the month

In the greenhouse

Attend carefully to all watering. Tomatoes can be given liquid fertiliser at least twice a week when carrying a good crop. Side-shoot regularly, but remove leaves only round trusses that are ripening.

Cucumbers need regular overhead sprayings with clear water.

Shade is essential for cucumbers, but only needed for tomatoes where sun strikes direct around the middle of the day.

Ventilate to keep a change of air, but close down by early evening if cool.

Outside

Plant out French and runner beans, marrows, outdoor cucumbers, tomatoes and sweet corn without protection after the first week of the month.

Plant celery, and water in.

Sow last of peas, using an early variety.

Earth-up late potatoes.

Pinch tops out of broad beans to deter blackfly.

Give early planted cabbage and cauliflowers a pinch of sulphate of ammonia per plant, keeping it off the leaves.

Plant out leeks.

Reviewing the situation

This is the time – nicely into the season – when we can do ourselves a bit of good by looking both forwards and backwards over the veg list. It is not too late to remedy some of our omissions and mistakes, and we can at the same time remind ourselves of things we have still to do.

Artichoke, globe
A mulch around these feeds them and keeps the weeds down, and don't forget that the small flower buds have to be taken off if you want that one good big one on the top.

Artichoke, Jerusalem
A mulch if you like, but nothing else.

Aubergine
Plant these outside now, but they need a warm protected spot. Pinch the tops out when 12in (30cm) high. Plants inside will be setting fruit, and need plenty of water and liquid food. Watch for whitefly.

Beans, broad
Too late to sow these now. Pinch the tops out of plants with a good set of flowers, and dust or spray against blackfly.

Beans, French
A few brushwood sticks among growing plants will help to keep them upright in exposed places. June sowings grow and come into bearing very quickly.

Beans, runner
It is safe to set out those inside-raised plants now, and still time to sow seeds outside. Watch for slugs and blackfly, and encourage climbing with a tie or two if necessary.

Beetroot
Seedlings must be thinned carefully to 3–4in (8–10cm) apart. A light sprinkling of sulphate of ammonia along the sides of the row will push them along. A nice time to sow now for maincrop or later pulling.

Broccoli, sprouting
It's a bit late for sowing the seeds of either the purple or the white varieties now, and if you haven't got your own plants coming on, be looking out for some. The best planting time is around the end of June. Can follow potatoes.

Brussels sprouts
Much too late for seed sowing. Plants must be set out as soon as possible. Any plants that were set out earlier will benefit from a slight earthing-up when they are nicely away. Watch for fly, caterpillars and slugs in wet weather.

Cabbage, spring
Should be hearting up now, but cut and use whether they are or not. Next year's seeds are sown in about six weeks' time.

Cabbage, early summer
A pinch of sulphate of ammonia to each plant will push these on if you're waiting for them.

Cabbage, late summer and autumn
Set out plants of these now and water in to get them started.

Cabbage, savoy
As above.

Cabbage, January King
Still just about time to sow seeds of these, but plants ready in a week or two's time would be better.

Calabrese
Too late for seeds. Plant in the next week or two.

Carrots
Earliest sowings will soon be ready for pulling. Thin out seedlings needed to grow on. This is a time to sow for both pulling in the autumn and a storing crop. Use a soil insecticide along rows to deter carrot fly, and watch for aphis on the leaves.

Cauliflower, summer
Watch for the earliest planted to be making flowers – they soon go past their best. A pinch of

sulphate of ammonia will put weight on later-set-out plants. Still time to plant more.

Cauliflower, winter
Just about time to sow seeds of these, but plants in the next two weeks would be better. Take precautions against aphis, caterpillars, slugs and root fly with all brassicas in the next two months. Birds may be a nuisance with new plants and seedlings.

Celeriac
Set plants out now and water in.

Celery
Just right to set out plants of all varieties now. Always water in and keep watered. Watch for a type of leafminer. Pick off affected leaves, and spray or dust with derris. Soot and soot water are also helpful.

Chicory
Thin out seedlings to 8–9in (20–23cm) apart.

Cucumbers, indoor
Water fruiting plants copiously over both leaves and roots. Shade and keep as warm as possible at night. Pinch off end of shoots at two leaves past fruit to encourage new growths. Set out new plants. Still time to sow seeds.

Cucumbers, outdoors
Time to set out plants in prepared positions, and keep watered. Seeds can also be sown where they are to grow.

Kohl Rabi
Thin out early sowings to 4–6in (10–15cm) apart. Sow again for succession.

Leeks
Too late to sow seeds. Plants from straw to pencil thickness can be set out at any time in the next six weeks. No pests to worry about, but must be kept clear of weeds. Follow early potatoes nicely.

Lettuce
Keep up the successional sowings of summer varieties, but from now on you can't rely on transplanting the seedlings. Sow thinly, thin out and throw away the surplus. Water the drills before sowing if dry. Lettuce respond well to liquid fertiliser.

Marrows and courgettes
Set plants out now and water in. Seeds can also be sown *in situ.* Water is essential.

Onions
Japanese varieties from last year's sowings will soon be ready to harvest. Dig up when tops start to dry off. Maincrop from plants, seed or sets should be growing away well. Keep weed-free, but avoid damaging the tops. Spray with a fungicide if mildew was experienced last year, or at first signs. Sow White Lisbon now for autumn salads.

Parsnip
Too late to sow seeds. Should be growing strongly now and must be thinned out if necessary.

Peas
Clear out old haulms as soon as possible and plant brassicas along the undug rows. Protect later sowings from birds, and make a last sowing in the next week or so of an 'early' variety. Water and liquid feed are most beneficial when the pods have appeared. Spray flowers with derris to deter pea maggot.

Peppers
Exactly as aubergines.

Potatoes
It's worth trying out 'earlies' every few days now, by burrowing to the roots without disturbing them too much. Fork over and clear ground well when digging to plant fresh crops. Lates should be moulded up when 12in (30cm) high, sprinkling fertiliser along the rows first if thought necessary. Water greatly improves the yield.

Radish
Can still be sown for succession in watered drills.

Shallots
Don't damage the tops at this time of the year by hoeing or weeding. Leave well alone, and they will start to die down next month.

Spinach
Too late to sow summer spinach. Spinach beet can be sown next month for autumn, winter and spring cropping. Seakale beet can be sown now, thinning out seedlings to 9–12in (23–30cm) apart.

Swedes
Most people sow too early. This is just the right time.

Sweet Corn
Set plants out now in groups 12in (30cm) apart. Must have warmth and sunshine. Too late to sow seeds.

Tomatoes, indoor
Keep well watered and fed, ventilate freely, keep side-shooted and supported. Lower leaves may be removed, but only from around ripening fruit. Shading of the tops of plants may be necessary on hot, dry days. Watch for whitefly.

Tomatoes, outdoor
Plant out now in warm positions if possible. Bush varieties may need a little shoot selection where growth is thick and close. Give liquid fertiliser when fruits start to form.

Turnips
Use early-sown varieties quickly as they soon become 'hot' and tough. Summer varieties can be sown until the end of this month. Watch for flea beetle boring holes in the seed leaves. Dust with derris to prevent.

Cucumbers

You don't need a greenhouse to grow cucumbers of the ridge type. Grow them in the open on low mounds of rich soil, spaced 30in (75cm) apart, or on continuous ridges at similar spacing for larger supplies.

1 Take out planting holes in a sunny, but sheltered, part of the garden. Make them about 12–18in (30–45cm) wide and deep.

2 Ridge cucumbers are heavy feeders, so fork in plenty of well-rotted manure or compost into the base of the hole; mix some with the in-fill soil as well.

3 Fill the hole with this enriched soil, then top this with fine compost 2–3in (5–8cm) deep to form a low mound. Don't make the mound too high, or it will dry out quickly.

5 If you've raised your cucumbers in the greenhouse, these can be planted out after hardening off in a cold frame. In cold areas, delay planting until the middle of the month.

4 Seeds can still be sown for late cropping. Sow about 1in (2–3cm) deep in small groups, which will later be thinned to leave the strongest seedling.

6 Give both seeds and plants the protection of a small cloche until they get established. Water the soil, but try to keep moisture off the plants themselves.

Take a tip . . .

- There isn't the soot about that there used to be, but if you can get hold of any, it's a valuable commodity in the veg garden. It has a certain fertiliser value (though this is very variable), but it is also a great pest deterrent. The soot must be a few months old when it is used, and preferably kept outside and weathered. Then it can be scattered thinly over the top of celery, onions, carrots and brassicas as a barrier against the fly that attacks them all. The soot can also be put in a bag, sunk in a tub of water, and the diluted water sprayed over almost any crop with benefit.

- Mid-June is the time to stop all cutting of asparagus, even the 'fern' tops that go so well in flower vases. It is these green tops that help to build-up next year's crowns. A top dressing 3–4in (7–10cm) thick of manure or compost will help in this direction.

Start right with leeks

The most difficult part of growing leeks is in producing good plants in time for setting out. Once established in their permanent positions, they are little trouble since they are not subject to pest or disease attack.

They are bone hardy too, and unaffected by frost and snow. This makes them almost a sure thing for the winter, and particularly useful because they do not have to be dug up and stored, but can be taken from the ground just as needed, even during the worst of the weather.

There are three things however that must be right if you want good leeks.

First, the ground. They do like rich, well-manured ground. It doesn't have to be specially prepared for them. In fact they follow early potatoes very well, if the ground was manured well for the potatoes.

Second, the time of setting out. They must be settled in in time to do most of their growing before the bad weather starts. They stop growing in November in any case, big or small, and the longer they've had – all other things being equal – the bigger they'll be by then. Mid-July planting is as late as you should go.

The third thing is the size of the individual plants when they are put out. Small plants make small leeks; big plants make big leeks.

The time of sowing the seed, and their rate of growth, is what controls this. In a seed row, there will always be plants of different thicknesses. And these, if mixed when set out, will always be a mixed lot. They never even up.

It is always best then, when the time comes, to lift them all with a fork and plant only the best. You may have to make two grades, but if so, plant them separately and don't bother to plant the smallest – they'll be a waste of time and room.

The ideal size is from straw to pencil thickness, and the ideal planting time is as soon as ever they have reached that size. If they reach it in June, you are well away. If it's in July, then you're still OK.

Leek planting is different from anything else. They must have a good length of white to be worth having, and that is achieved by keeping this part dark. Exhibitors wrap them up in some way, but for ordinary use it is enough to make a deep planting hole, so that 9in (23cm) or so of the plant is underground.

This is another reason why good plants are essential. It is no good dropping a 6in (15cm) long plant into a 9in (23cm) deep hole – it may despair of ever reaching the light and just fade away.

If they are 10–12in (25–30cm) long, the tops are just above ground, and with their roots down in the cool moist soil below they are almost sure to get away quickly.

The surface of the soil is best if it is trodden and raked smooth, as this enables a clean hole to be made with a dibber or bar.

The plants are dropped in, making sure they reach the bottom, and there is no need to push any soil in, although a spot or two of water carefully trickled in helps them recover from the move.

Support your tomatoes

Don't leave tomatoes to flop before providing adequate support for them. If yours are in growing-bags, wires and soft twine can be used. Otherwise, use canes and twine. Keep the plants growing healthily by controlling pests and maintain vigour by feeding.

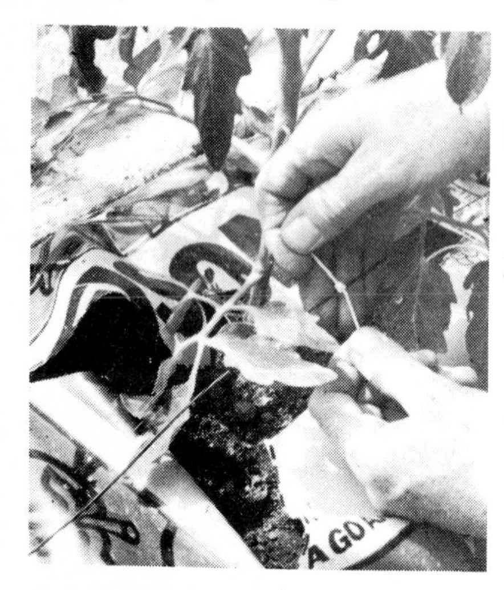

1 If you don't have a proprietary growing-bag support, fix plastic-covered wire along the tops of the bags and tie soft garden twine to this at the base of the tomato plants.

2 Tie the other end of the twine to a support wire stretched across the roof of the greenhouse. Allow extra twine for running up the roof to support further growth.

3 Gently twist the tomato shoots round the twine, taking care not to damage the foliage or flower trusses.

4 Remove the side-shoots as soon as they are large enough to rub out easily. Left to develop, they rob the plant of energy that should be used for growth of the leading shoots.

5 Keep a sharp watch for signs of whitefly (they look like tiny white moths) and control them with a proprietary pesticide.

6 Begin to feed tomatoes in growing bags as soon as the first flower truss has set fruit. Always make sure the compost is moist before applying fertiliser.

Winter veg

Brussels sprouts
The best bet for winter greenstuff is, without a doubt, a good row or two of brussels sprouts. There's no other veg that can be turned to over such a long period. And that time is through the worst part of the year, from November to March.

But to do any good, they must be planted soon – this month for sure. Don't rush out and buy a packet of seeds. It's too late to sow seeds of brussels and you'd be throwing money away. But do anything and everything you can to get hold of some well-grown plants.

They should be strong, around 6–10in (15cm) tall, and they want to be back in the ground, 2–3ft (60–90cm) apart all ways, and watered in, before they have a chance to wither and dry up.

Cabbage
Only one other winter green approaches the usefulness of brussels in hardiness and the period over which it is available. That is the cabbage January King and its near relation, the smaller January Prince. A row of plants put in now could be cut as they hearted up, from November until February.

Keep an eye on them for signs of bursting, but even this doesn't make them inedible. Again, you want plants now rather than seed, although it is possible with these to sow the seed thinly in a row in June, and thin them out to 15in (38cm) apart.

Savoys, winter cauliflowers, broccoli and kale
The rest of the winter greens can be conveniently divided into two kinds: those that are not quite hardy and have to be cut or used before the worst of the weather, usually by January, and those that are able to stand through the winter as partly developed plants, which sprout and produce their crop in the spring.

The first group includes mainly cabbages of some kind, while the second lot are the winter cauliflowers, sprouting broccoli and kales. As before, plants set out this month are a far better bet than seeds.

Included in the first group are the late savoys. Make sure that any plants you obtain are late varieties and Ormskirk Late and Rearguard are the sort of names to look for.

The late cabbages in this group are those useful, generally white-hearted varieties.

Winter Salad and Hidena are examples of this type, and the beauty of them is that it is possible to pull them up when they are fully developed in early winter, and if they are hung up with stem and root attached, they will keep quite fresh and crisp for a couple of months at least.

No time must be wasted in getting these late cabbages in and away. They must make their hearts before the weather turns bad, so they need watering in at planting time. If the ground is at all suspect they will need a boosting fertiliser halfway through their growing season. Planting distance for all these is 15–18in (38–45cm) all ways.

The plants in the final group are not quite so demanding about planting time. It is still rather late to sow seeds of the sprouting broccolis, kales and winter cauliflowers, but if plants can be set out by the end of July, they have time to grow to a fair size before they stop growing for the winter. They should not be given any kind of boost this side of Christmas. But a quick-acting fertiliser applied in February, will push along the new spring growth and that is, of course, the part we eat.

Winter cauliflowers, which used to be called heading broccoli, heart up at different times from January to June, according to variety. Only in very favoured districts is it worth trying to grow the January/February kinds, but varieties like St George (March/April), Progress (May) and Juno (June) are some of the most valuable of all veg.

The other winter veg to plant in the next few weeks is leeks. They aren't to everyone's taste, but are reliable because they are bone hardy and almost pest and disease free.

July

Go walkabout! This is the month to spend a lot of time strolling round the veg plot. Not for the exercise, but to spot all the numerous little jobs that need doing.

The weeds will be obvious, so take a hoe with you. You'll have to look more closely for pests, but they'll be there in abundance, hiding in the foliage. Declare instant war on them – you simply can't afford to show any mercy.

You will also spot more pleasant jobs to do. Taking the side-shoots off tomatoes, for example. This ensures that the fruit, when it eventually appears, will be a decent size. The same goes for runner beans. When the plants have wound themselves to the top of the poles, pinch out the growing points so that all the energy of the plants is diverted into producing good pods.

Watch onions and shallots in case they show any signs of running to seed. As soon as you see any small pods forming, nip them off, otherwise the stem will harden and the bulbs won't form properly.

Finally, remember to keep everything well watered during dry spells. It's a bind, but the job must be done.

Jobs for the month

In the greenhouse

Watch for whitefly building up in the greenhouse. Use specific whitefly sprays and fumigate regularly.

Red spider attacks cucumbers in particular. Regular spraying with clear water over and under the leaves will keep them away.

Take off male flowers – those without fruit behind them – as soon as you can recognise them. Continue to feed tomatoes. Damp down the floors during day to provide humidity.

Outside

Sow turnips and swedes, and as seedlings appear, dust them with derris to protect from flea beetle.

Sow lettuce for succession, but thin out only. Do not transplant. Sow early carrots for pulling young. Sow parsley for winter use.

Plant late savoys, winter cauliflowers and cabbage and sprouting broccoli.

Water and feed outdoor cucumbers, tomatoes, marrows. Runner beans and celery will need water in dry weather.

Spray or dust all greens with derris to deter caterpillars.

Protect peas against pests

If you want plump, sweet green peas for the table, protect the plants against pests like the pea moth, which lays its eggs on the developing pods, and provide adequate moisture to keep the crop growing steadily.

1 Some of the short-stemmed peas may not have been given stick supports, but prevent the wind blowing the haulms over by running twine down either side of the rows.

2 If you want succulent peas, make sure the plants are well supplied with water in dry spells. And remember, one thorough soaking is better than lots of sprinklings.

3 Mulching the rows with compost or moist peat will help to conserve soil moisture during the summer. Apply after watering the rows.

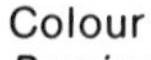

Colour

Previous page Cauliflower 'Snow King' – looks like the fallen snow, doesn't it? Produces large, tasty heads in just over 2½ months after planting, making it an incredibly fast grower (Picture: Ian and Stuart Unwin)

Above left Sweet corn 'Northern Belle' – recommended because, in trials, it has produced such a consistent and heavy crop of large ears. The flavour's good and, of course, it freezes well (Picture: Thompson & Morgan)

Above right Pepper 'Mexican Chilli' – hot little devils, these. Spicy too. You need a greenhouse to grow them, and when they mature you simply dry and grind the fruits and you have chilli powder (Picture: Thompson & Morgan)

Below left Runner bean 'Crusader' – an excellent exhibition variety with the pods growing to over 20in (50cm) long. They snap easily, crop well and taste good. Yes, big is beautiful (Picture: Thompson & Morgan)

Below right Pepper 'Gold Topaz' – first there was white beetroot, now yellow peppers! Apart from its novel colour, it's distinctive for its unusually mild yet spicy flavour, which should suit all tastes (Picture: Thompson & Morgan)

4 Don't let pea moth ruin the crop. To control this pest, spray with Fentro as first flowers open and repeat two weeks later.

How potatoes help clean up your soil

If you've planted potatoes this year with the idea that they will help to clean up a patch of ground, it's important that you play your own part.

The tops of the plants do have a smothering effect on weeds that deters them quite a bit, but it's the three disturbances of the soil that do more than anything else to conclude the trick successfully.

The first is the digging at planting time. The second is the hoeing and earthing-up of the plants, and the third, the most important, is when the crop is dug.

With earlies in particular, this final moving of the ground comes at a time when weeds are vulnerable. The soil should be thoroughly moved and disturbed at that time, and rubbish of all sorts ruthlessly dug out. A further point is that there is still plenty of time for the inevitable crop of new seedlings to germinate, and Dutch hoeing in late summer and autumn will kill them by the million, if it is done on a dry sunny day.

A technique of digging potatoes is needed so that the ground is thoroughly moved and so that it is not trodden on afterwards. People develop ways of their own, but one of the best ways is to straddle the plants with the row behind you.

Take the first one or two forkfuls of soil away from the front of the plant to leave a hole, and then, with the fork, thrust well down and under and heave the whole root into this hole with the roots exposed as much as possible.

Riddling it through with the fork brings the potatoes and the rubbish to the surface. Every bit of ground is then dug until the next plant is reached, and the sequence continues.

Keep it reasonably level, and have something to put the tops and the weeds into, to save walking on the ground afterwards to collect them. Never leave the rubbish on top of the ground for long. Some of the weeds might develop and shed seeds – groundsel is particularly liable to do this – and the haulms themselves will harbour slugs and woodlice.

Ground that has been cleared of earlies can well be used for another crop. But how you use it, or whether you use it at all, rather depends on what type of soil it is.

Heavy ground just reclaimed, for instance, might be impossible to break down well enough in a dry season to sow small seeds, or even in some cases to set plants. Where soil is like this, it is far better to leave it, hoeing and forking it during the later summer, with a view to making it better for next year.

Riddling through the soil with a fork brings the potatoes to the surface.

Successional carrots

Successional carrots will need thinning to get good-sized roots but remember, any soil disturbance or the odour of crushed foliage is liable to attract the female carrot flies, which are only too willing to lay eggs near the crop. These hatch out into small grubs that bore into the roots.

1 Keep weeds down between carrot rows by hoeing but hand-weed in the rows to disturb the soil as little as possible.

2 Allow ½in (13mm) between bulk-crop carrots, but for large roots thin in three stages to allow a final spacing of 4in (10cm) between plants.

3 Avoid bruising foliage, burn thinnings and water immediately after to settle soil. Thin on dull days or after sunset to discourage root fly activity.

4 Applying soil insecticide to the seedling rows will also help to deter carrot-root flies from laying eggs.

Tomato pests

It's strange that of all the trials and tribulations we get with our tomatoes, very few of them are caused by pests.

Diseases and disorders come thick and fast, but the balance is restored, thank goodness, by the absence, or at least the scarcity, of regular hordes of mocradytes. (All right, what's your word for a collection of creepy-crawlies?)

There are, of course, cases where damage comes from unlikely sources. Various caterpillars have a go sometimes, but consistent tomato pests are very few.

Worst of all must be the greenhouse whitefly, and even this is generally brought into the house on some other plant to migrate quickly to the tomatoes. It has a weakening effect on the plants, but the sticky mess it leaves and the resulting moulds that grow on it are the biggest trouble. It means that every fruit has to be washed before it can be used.

The trouble is that insecticides will only kill the adult flies. The eggs and the larvae, which are the in-between stage, are unharmed and continue to hatch out. Persistent use of the specially formulated whitefly insecticides until the pest is cleared is necessary, and by far the

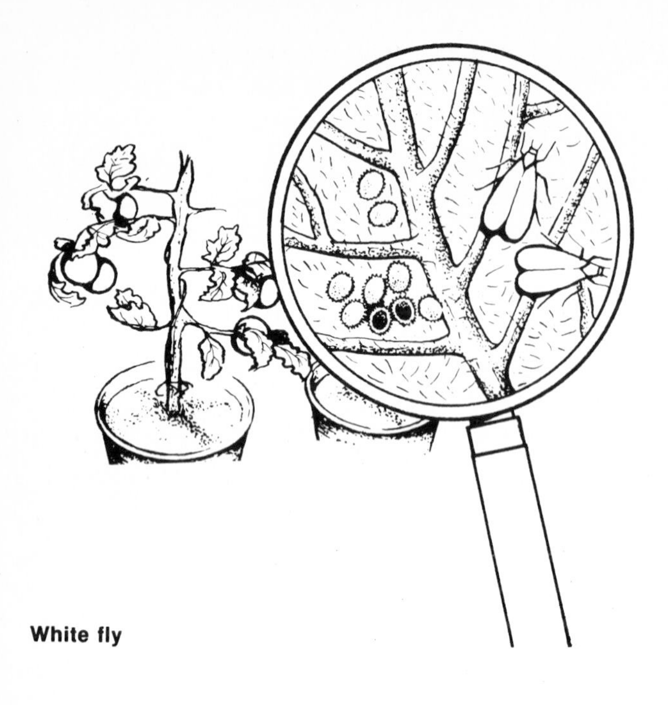

White fly

best way is to keep an aerosol of it handy and to use it at least every seven days. Whitefly can also be cleared by introducing into the greenhouse another insect, a parasite wasp, *Encarsia formosa*. This small mite lives on the whitefly larvae, and will effectively clear a house in a short time.

Red spider is a pest that bothers many kinds of plants only when the conditions are favourable. If a degree of humidity is kept, and the plants are regularly sprayed with clear water, especially under the leaves, they never get out of hand. But in hot dry conditions they quickly breed and spread to the tomatoes. The leaves then take on a silvery grey look, the plants stop growing and, in severe cases, webs are formed in the tips and over fruit trusses.

When they get as bad as this, there is little that can be done. Repeated sprayings with derris are a good and certainly as safe as anything, but there is nothing to beat clear water used as a deterrent. Prevention, in the case of red spider, is far easier than cure.

Various caterpillars attack tomatoes at times, but by far the most serious is that of the tomato moth. Even this is not common but it sometimes seems to invade a district and cause a lot of local trouble. When quite small, the caterpillars feed on the back of the leaves and eventually, as they grow, eat all the green parts, leaving just the skeleton of veins. When fully grown they are more than 1in (2–3cm) long, and at that stage will burrow into the stems, causing collapse, and even make holes in the fruit.

It pays to keep a watch for any skeletonising of the leaves as this is generally the first sign. Then an immediate spray with derris – still one of the best caterpillar killers – must be carried out. The fully grown caterpillars are green to brown and have a yellow line, bordered with black and white spots, along their backs.

By the time they have reached this stage all the damage will have been done, but this description should help you identify the pest.

Tomato moth

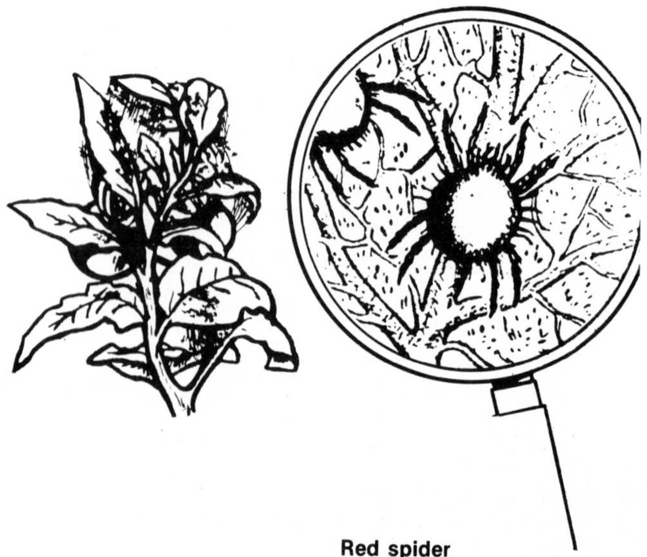

Red spider

Sowing spring cabbage

From now until mid-August is the time to sow spring cabbages to give transplants during September and October. In the south, delay sowing until next month. Try Wheeler's Imperial if you only have a small plot. Other varieties include Durham Elf, Golden Acre and Early Offenham.

1 Apply a general balanced fertiliser before raking over the seed bed to get a level fine sowing tilth.

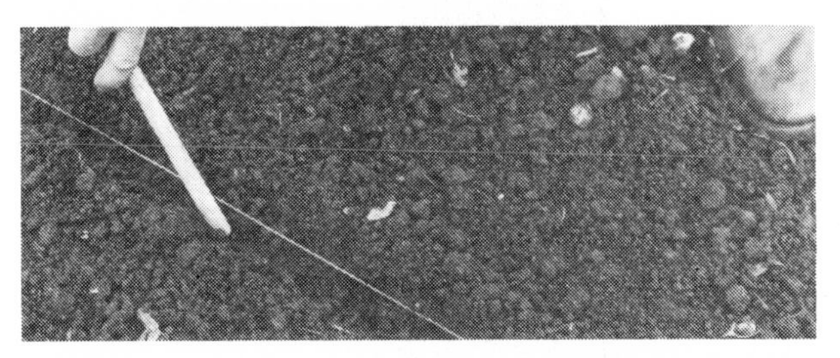

2 Use a line or rake handle to give straight lines, and draw out a shallow drill. A short row will give more than adequate transplants.

3 Sow the seed thinly and evenly down the drill to avoid overcrowding in the seedling stage.

4 Cover the seeds by raking over drill lightly or shuffling soil in with your shoes. Keep seed bed moist to encourage even germination.

Taking care with Japanese onions

If you've ever had words with your wife or husband for wanting to pull up a couple of your best onions in July to save buying some, and you can't bear to see one go because it'll spoil the look of the best bed you've had for years, sow some Japanese onions in August.

They ripen and are harvested in late June and July, and fill the gap marvellously between last year's stored onions finishing and this year's being ready.

If you regularly manage a fair bed of conventional spring-sown onions, you won't need a lot of these in-betweeners, but a row or two comes in handy, both for pulling green in early spring, and to grow on into half-pounders or so by the end of June.

The new kinds of Japanese onions with the oriental names – Kaizuka, Imai Yellow, Senshyu – and the more conventional sounding Express Yellow, are a big advance.

They are hardier, easier to grow because they come through the winter better, less inclined to bolt to seed, earlier to mature, and will keep, if you want to keep them, from harvesting in July until Christmas.

However, we must get a few things straight.

First, although heavy ground shouldn't put you off trying them, they are more likely to be killed through the winter by being water-logged than by anything else, and a well-drained patch gives them the best chance.

Second, the time of sowing is critical. They

must be big enough when the bad weather starts and they stop growing to stand through the winter. Yet they must not be too big or they will bolt in the spring. The aim should be to have plants about 8in (20cm) high by the end of October.

The best guide is this. In Scotland and the north, sow in the first week in August. In the south and south-east sow in the third week, in the Midlands and East Anglia sow in the second week, and in the mild south-west the last week, or even the first week in September should do.

Seeds must germinate and come through without any check, of course, or observing these strict sowing times will be useless. To encourage them, make a fine seed bed, draw 1in (2–3cm) deep drills 12in (30cm) apart, trickle water along the bottom so that they're muddy, sow on that mud about ½in (13mm) apart, cover with dry soil, and rake over lightly and evenly.

They should be showing through in from seven to ten days.

Third, don't try growing them on poor ground. They want a good fertile soil (such as where a good crop of early potatoes has been lifted) and raked into the surface in the ground-preparing process, 4–6oz (110–170gm) of Growmore or similar to 1sqyd (1sqm).

They'll also want nitrogen, either sulphate of ammonia or nitro-chalk, once or twice in February, March and April, at about ½oz a yard (15gm per metre) run of plants. This is to replace the nitrogen that is almost sure to be washed out of the ground during the winter rains.

Fourth, it's most important to keep them free of weeds. Don't be tempted into thinking that weeds will help to protect them from the cold. They might to a degree, but they're better off without them.

Thin them out when they're big enough to eat, but don't transplant them.

Fifth, remember these onions are grown for using, not for keeping. Start on them in June/July and aim to use them all by Christmas.

Transplanting sprouting broccoli

Sprouting broccoli, like winter cauliflowers, prefers a firm soil, so there's no need to dig over ground that becomes vacant after harvesting summer crops. Just hoe in fertiliser and remove any persistent weeds. Treating the transplants with calomel will help to discourage club root disease.

1 As ground becomes vacant after cropping, hoe in general fertiliser or 2oz (50gm) superphosphate and 1oz (25gm) sulphate of potash per square yard. Remove any weeds as you go.

2 The night before you intend to transplant broccoli, water the seedling rows to make lifting easier and prevent excess damage to roots.

3 Take out a shallow drill down the plot using a line. If more than one row is needed, space out 24in (60cm) apart.

4 Plant out 24in (60cm) apart in the rows, treating the hole and roots of transplants with calomel dust, or dipping roots into a slurry made up of calomel and water.

5 Firm the transplants in well, using knuckles or trowel handle, then water in thoroughly.

Lettuce – hints for big hearts

One of the main attractions of growing your own vegetables is that they are better than you can buy – tastier, fresher and generally better quality. Or at least, that's the general idea.

But it's surprising how often this isn't true of one of the simplest of them all – lettuce.

Many people say that they cannot seem to grow lettuce as good, and, nine times out of ten, they mean as 'hearted', as they can get from the shops. Looking around the gardens it is quite true.

The main reason is pretty basic. Lettuce suffers because it's too easy. The seeds are cheap and plentiful enough to use without much concern.

We know, almost with certainty, that if we put lettuce seed in, almost anyhow and almost anywhere, it will come up, and because almost any lettuce leaf is eatable, we know we shall get something from it. It therefore tends to get shoved into holes and corners where we wouldn't think of trying to grow onions, say, or carrots or cauliflowers, and then we grumble because the plants don't turn out first-class.

It applies most, of course, to the mid-season and late sowings. The first sowings of the season, made in March and April, are put in when there's plenty of room, and when we're keen enough and not too busy to keep them hoed, protected from slugs and birds, and, above all, thinned out to give them space to grow. Or it may be that we've set out plants that we've raised in boxes or even bought and, bearing in mind what they've cost us, we make a bit more fuss of them.

But when it comes to sowing for succession, we may be pushed for time and not have allowed room for them. They don't get a good spot or the proper attention, and this is when they don't turn out too well.

Generally it isn't the soil that's wrong. They grow biggest and best in rich, well-manured ground, of course, but almost any well-cultivated soil will grow lettuce.

What must be right to get them hearted is the light and the spacing. They won't heart-up under trees or overshadowed by potato tops or brussels sprout plants. They'll grow and make leaves, but they won't make a solid heart. They won't even heart-up properly in the shade of a wall or fence. Full all-round light is essential.

Of course they won't heart up if they haven't the space to grow. Too often in gardens, lettuce are sown and not thinned out. Perhaps the grower won't make time to do the job, or perhaps he doesn't like throwing thinnings away. But if this is the case he mustn't be surprised if he is only able to cut leaves. Give a lettuce full light and full room to grow, and it will almost invariably produce a heart of some kind, even if it isn't the best lettuce in the world.

One other thing. Although lettuces transplant well at the beginning of the season, they aren't such sure things after the middle of June, and in summer it's best to sow them, thin them out, and leave those you want undisturbed. Sow them thinly, make sure they come up by watering along the drills first, and if it hurts you to throw the thinnings away, thin them out when they're very small and showing only the seed leaves. That way it doesn't seem so wasteful.

There's still time, by the way, to sow summer lettuce and get them hearted. Any sown in August may well need a cloche put over them in late September, for a bit of protection, but it isn't always necessary. Of course, remember that late August and early September is sowing time for the special breed of winter lettuce that stands the winter and hearts up in early spring next year.

It's always best with all summer sowings of seeds to water the drills to ensure quick and even germination. Immediately the water has drained away, sow the seed and cover with dry soil. This is the way to test lettuce for hearting. Never squeeze them from the sides, for this may well start decay if they have to be left.

Take a tip . . .

- Potato blight shows as brown blotches on the leaves and stems, and it generally appears in July. But it's best not to wait to see it, but to spray with fungicide as a preventive. Bordeaux mixture or orthocide used at 10-day intervals through July should keep it away. Remember, blight also attacks outdoor tomatoes, so spray these at the same time.

- Perpetual spinach is quite hardy—it will stand the winter and give a picking at almost any time. Sown in July, there will be leaves to pick in autumn, possibly in winter and certainly in the early spring. Sow in rows 12in (30cm) apart and thin the plants to 9in (23cm) apart.

- If you want to get rid of an old mint bed, the best time to dig it up is in July. Throw out the old roots, pick out all the pieces you can, and keep disturbing the soil over the next few weeks. This is much better than trying to do it when the ground is wet in the autumn or winter, and more likely to kill it than if done in the spring.

- Don't be tempted to sow spring cabbage seed in any hole or corner. The plants tend to be twisty and leggy at the best of times, and if they are raised in the shade, they will be worse than ever, and very awkward to transplant. Give them a spot in full light, and above all, sow thinly. They should go in before the second week in August.

- If you've any aubergines outside, don't be misled into thinking they'll stand up for themselves at all times. As the large fruits form, they are in danger of being blown over and it's wise to give them all a stake and tie.

August

Think ahead! It may still be high summer, but now's the time to start thinking about next year's crops. Indeed, you can sow some this month, over-wintering them in the veg plot for cutting at the start of the next season.

Two of the most popular are winter lettuce (which you sow now for April cutting) and spring cabbage. Seed of the latter sown in August will produce healthy little plants by October, and these can then be transplanted into their growing positions. Be careful about the sort of lettuce seed you buy. Only hardy varieties are strong enough to survive the winter, so make sure you choose the right type.

Another crop worth sowing now is Japanese onions. They will be ready for harvesting next June or July.

As for your established crops, continue to go walkabout on your plot, carrying out any jobs that need doing. One really important task is to 'stop' outdoor tomatoes. This means pinching-out the tops of the plants after each plant has formed four or five trusses of fruit. If you fail to do this, the plants will produce small tomatoes.

Early peas, broad beans and early new potatoes will be coming to an end, but these will soon be replaced by tomatoes, sweet corn, runner beans, cucumbers and marrows.

Jobs for the month

In the greenhouse

Pinch the growing tips from tomatoes after six to eight trusses have been made. Remove lower leaves as fruit ripens.

Cut cucumbers while still young and top-dress plants with fresh compost.

Outside

Sow Japanese onions for harvesting next June/ July.

Sow winter lettuce for April cutting.

Sow spring-cabbage seed for transplanting in October.

Harvest shallots, exposing them to sunshine so that they ripen.

Lift and store early-sown beetroot.

Pick French and runner beans regularly.

Spray potatoes with fungicide early in the month to prevent scab attack.

Sowing turnips

Turnips provide a tasty addition to both cooked and cold meals, particularly when pulled young. Sown now, they will provide roots for immediate use or for storing from mid-October, and those sown late in the month will give a crop of leaves that can be used as greens.

1 Pull turnip roots when still fairly small to get the best flavour. These can be cooked whole or used raw in salads.

2 To give large roots for storing or freezing, sow now on ground cleared of other summer crops like peas or spinach. Lightly dig over and remove all weeds.

3 Apply a general fertiliser at the rate of 3–4oz per square yard (90–120gm per sqm) and rake in, breaking down the soil into a fine sowing tilth.

4 If the soil is light, gently firm down by treading, then sow thinly into shallow drills. A ¼oz (7gm) of seed will sow about 30ft (say 9m) run of drill.

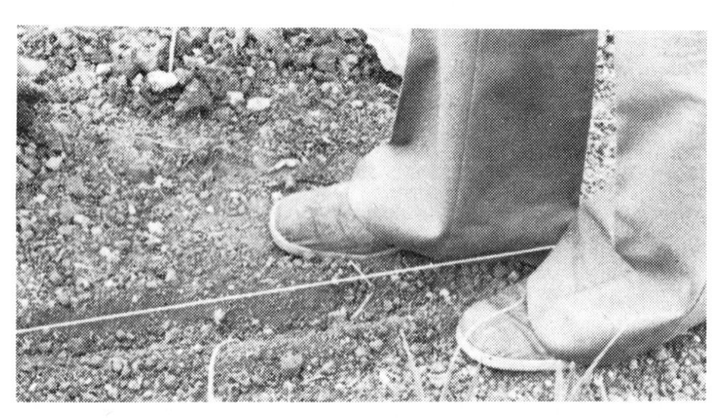

5 Cover the seeds by drawing soil over with the rake or shuffling it in with your feet, and gently firm with the rake-head or by treading.

6 At this time of the year, it's important to keep seed rows moist to get good germination. Thin the seedlings as soon as they are large enough to handle.

Cabbage – make sure you grow the right types

A beginner at the gardening game may not know the difference between summer cabbage and spring cabbage.

Those known as spring cabbage are sown in a seed bed in August and transplanted into their growing positions in October; they stand through the winter as small plants, and grow on into edible size in April and May.

Summer cabbage are sown and do all their growing in one year.

It's not a bit of use thinking that one type will do as well as the other. They are distinct and must be sown and grown at their correct times.

So sow spring cabbage seeds during the first three weeks of August – early in this period in the north, later in the south.

Well-known varieties are Durham Elf, Flower of Spring and Wheeler's Imperial, but there are others. The main thing is to get the right type – *spring* cabbage. The variety doesn't matter so much.

Alternatively, of course, there are always plants for sale in October, ready to set out, and as long as you can trust your supplier, a score or two of these will save you the bother of sowing seeds.

A picture to pinpoint the difference between spring and summer cabbages. On the left: summer cabbage plants raised in the greenhouse and just planted out in April. On the right: spring cabbages planted out the previous autumn and just starting to heart-up after standing through the winter.

Leeks – a feed will help

It's getting late in the season for feeding vegetables, particularly with nitrogenous fertilisers, which tend to encourage soft growth that can be damaged by an early spell of bad weather. But leeks don't come into this category, and if they're a bit behind, a sprinkle of sulphate of ammonia will put weight on them without any risk.

They go on growing longer than most things and are able to make use of nitrogen, which is supplied by sulphate of ammonia, for some time yet.

Until late August, then, it's worth giving them some. But leeks are awkward things to get among and it's not worth risking damage to the leaves by treading on them as you edge between the rows. Wait until rain is actually falling and then go out and scatter about ½oz (15gm) over the top of a dozen or so leeks. This would burn the leaves if put on dry, so either it must be raining or the leaves must be sprayed over with water immediately afterwards.

The other advantage of putting it on this way is that it becomes immediately available to the plants, and its effects can be seen inside a week.

Should you be tempted to think that the winter greens could benefit by this treatment, don't try it. They would certainly be pushed along, but would be made soft and lush and more easily frost-damaged.

Leeks at this stage will benefit from a feed, even as late in the year as the end of August.

Looking after brassicas

This is the last chance for gardeners in the south to sow spring-cabbage varieties like Wheeler's Imperial and Offenham selections. Protect the lovely white cauliflower curds, and, if you've a freezer, put down some of the best where there's a glut and they are likely to go over.

1 Sow seeds of spring cabbage in the seed bed after raking down into a fine tilth. Use a line to draw out a shallow drill, sow thinly and evenly, and keep the seed bed moist.

2 Where kale has been sown to crop *in situ* (Hungry Gap), thin out to allow 15in (38cm) between the plants. Pentland Brig kale can still be transplanted into any space ground at the same spacing – water well in.

3 High winds can cause havoc to taller-growing brassicas, so to avoid toppling, earth up the stems of kale and brussels sprouts, which are especially vulnerable.

4 Maturing heads of cauliflowers can be discoloured by hot sun, so provide some protection by shading them with a leaf broken over the curds, or tie up some of the foliage.

Tomatoes – removing shoots and stopping

If you look at tomatoes in commercial greenhouses now, you often find that the leaves have been cut off almost to the tops of the plants, exposing the fruits to all the available light.

You might be tempted to go home and do the same thing to yours, in an attempt to push along the ripening. But you would almost certainly be wrong.

The nursery plants would be early planted, with the whole crop fully developed right to the top, and when they have reached this stage there's nothing wrong with leaf removal.

But if your plants are later and the fruit are still swelling, cutting off all the leaves is the surest way of stopping them going on swelling. The leaves are the 'factory' part of the plants, and the action of light on them produces the food on which the fruit depends. It is only when fruit development is complete that they can go.

This doesn't mean that you can't cut off any leaves at all. They gradually lose their manufacturing capabilities anyway. The deterioration sets in at the bottom of the plant and moves progressively upwards. This then is the clue.

As the individual trusses reach their full size, so they can do without the leaves below and immediately around them. As ripening starts only when the fruit reaches full size, this is a good guide.

The rule to follow is to take off leaves below and up to the ripening fruit, but not above it. The exception is where a large upper leaf hangs over a truss, completely excluding the light, and this can be cut back by about half.

To shorten some leaves, rather than remove them completely, is not a bad idea. The lowest leaves, particularly if they are beginning to turn yellow, will snap off completely right back to the stem, just with the pressure of the fingers. This can be taken as a sign that they have lost their usefulness.

Further up the plant, they don't snap off so easily, and it is then better to shorten them by cutting at some point with a sharp knife or secateurs.

The other necessary operation is the 'stopping' of the plants. This is the removal of the growing tip, so that the production of more stem leaves and trusses is stopped, and the saved energy goes into the existing fruit.

There is no fixed time when this should be done, but by now there is not much point in letting plants go on making growth which is not going to have time to produce mature fruit. Outside plants in particular should be stopped at once. So should plants growing inside where chrysanthemums are to be moved into their place in a few weeks' time.

Only if they are vigorous healthy plants, not in the way of anything else, and if they can be kept warm with artificial heat in the cold autumn nights, is there any point in letting them go on growing now.

Remember to pinch off the tip at a leaf, not at a fruit truss, and remember too that vigorous plants, when stopped, will tend to make a host of side-shoots that need removing.

Leaves should be removed from below and around mature fruit. The lower leaves can be taken off right back to the main stem. Higher up the plant, it is enough to shorten them by a third or a half. When the tip of the plant is pinched off, one leaf at least must be left above the last truss to go on drawing up energy.

September

Get 'em in! Suddenly it's early autumn and this is something of a turning point in the garden. The weather is still quite good and your veg plot should still be producing bountiful crops. But you must think ahead to the winter when you'll want plenty of produce in store.

So towards the end of the month, start harvesting whole crops rather than picking produce as and when you need it. Far and away the best and easiest way of storing vegetables is to use a home freezer. But if you haven't one, then many crops can be stored in a dry place such as the garden shed.

Onions should be strung, marrows suspended in nets and root crops such as carrots and turnips stored in boxes or trays. Root crops and potatoes can, of course, also be stored in clamps of soil in the garden.

You may have a problem with tomatoes. Given a worse than average summer, then much of your crop may not have ripened by the end of September. The answer here is to harvest them green and take them indoors to ripen. One really effective way of ripening them is to place one ripe tomato in an egg box with five green fruits, put the lid down, and within days they will have ripened.

Jobs for the month

In the greenhouse

Clear tomatoes and cucumbers by the middle of the month if chrysanthemums are to be moved in.

Fumigate with smoke pellets.

Use bare floor or staging to ripen shallots and onions.

Outside

Sow an early lettuce to cloche in October.

Harvest all onions.

Cut off tops of maincrop potatoes as they yellow and dig after ten days or so.

Put stakes to big brussels sprouts plants in exposed positions.

Pick green tomatoes and ripen indoors.

Cut all marrows and outdoor cucumbers.

Storing onions

The most convenient way to store onions is on a string. This way they look attractive in the kitchen and save valuable space in the shed. When removing the bulbs, start from the top.

1 Start by hanging a loop of strong string on a convenient hook.

2 Bring the bottom of the loop up to form two smaller loops and thread the onion foliage through.

3 Pull the string tight to secure the first bulb. Cut off the excess foliage.

4 Open up the two strings and place the foliage of the next bulb through the middle.

5 Twist the leaves around both strings and through the middle.

6 Continue in the same way, using the largest bulbs first and placing them so that they hide the string.

Facing up to winter

At any time now the crunch will come in the veg garden, and instead of looking for something new coming along, as we do all the summer, we are more concerned with conserving the things we already have and making the most of them.

The veg position in the coming winter and as far on as next April and May, is always touch-and-go. It pays to be sure we do the right things with anything we can keep.

No risks at all must be taken with potatoes. Make sure those that are put into store are sound. Put on one side, for immediate use, any you may have forked while digging or any with slug or other pest damage. If stored, these will almost certainly start to rot and set off others around them. Tubers with the common scab disease do keep quite successfully, although it is as well to use the worst of them first.

Sacks are the most convenient storage for most people, but make sure no light gets at the potatoes through them, and of course keep them in a frost-proof but cool place.

Carrots and beetroot are often lost in store because they are coddled too much. Over-dry and over-warm conditions cause them to shrivel, and this can happen even if they are stored in the conventional box of peat and sand.

They do not have to be kept inside. In fact, a good way of keeping them, if a suitable position is available, is to put a layer of sand or ashes 3–4in (7–10cm) deep against a wall or fence outside.

Put the carrots or beetroot on this, placing them carefully rather than tipping them, and cover them with the same material, or possibly peat, to a depth of at least 6in (15cm) all over.

This will run between them, especially after it has rained and more will then have to be added.

They do not have to be kept dry, but take care that there are no overhead drips from roofs, and that water does not remain standing but drains quickly away.

The hole made to take some out must be well mended each time to keep out hard frosts.

Don't forget that the beetroot must not be damaged at all, either at the top when removing the leaves, or at the 'tails'. If a beet's skin is damaged in any way it loses all its colour when boiled.

Whether onions keep well or not in store depends more on how they are grown than how they are kept. If they are well ripened and harvested, it is rare for anything to go wrong.

They will keep in fairly thick layers on a shelf, in a corner of the floor in a cold shed or garage, or in a spare bedroom or attic.

They can be stacked in tomato trays, made up into onion 'ropes', or hung in nets or even old stockings or tights. And of course much the same methods are ideal for shallots.

The turnip and swede family can be left in the ground and used as needed, except in the coldest districts. Here they may be lifted in October and kept buried outside in the same way as carrots and beetroot.

Celeriac is not quite as hardy and, except in warm sheltered places, is best lifted and stored, again outside under sand or ashes.

Chicory and seakale roots can be dug up as needed from Christmas, for forcing. Parsnips, although best left where they are for using as needed, can be dug up if in the way of winter cultivation, as they often are, put in a heap and covered with soil in another part of the garden.

Marrows are not as a rule grown as a winter vegetable. If there are any unused when the frosts come and they have to be picked, they will keep if they are ripe and fully mature.

The best way is to have them up in a net, ideally in a pantry or larder.

Colour

Above left Potato 'Pentland Javelin' – one of the most popular first early potatoes, this. Grows vigorously and crops heavily, and with its white skin and flesh has excellent cooking qualities (Picture: Thompson & Morgan)

Above right Dwarf bean 'Remus'—unusual inasmuch as it bears its pods *above* the foliage. This means that the beans grow and ripen faster because they get much more light and air than other varieties (Picture: Thompson & Morgan)

Below Lettuce 'Little Gem' – one of the best-tasting of all lettuces, this has a delicious sweet flavour. Just the thing to eat with an exotic fish dish . . . (Picture: Thompson & Morgan)

Setting spring cabbage

Spring-cabbage plants can be set out now, though if they are not yet big enough there is no hurry. Grow them in a sheltered part of the garden that was manured for a previous crop.

1 During a spell of dry weather, the plants are best set out in a drill to retain water.

2 Using a dibber, set the plants out at 9in (23cm) intervals with 18in (45cm) between rows.

3 Firm them in really well and give them a good watering after planting.

Colour
Cos Lettuce 'Lobjoits Green' – produces large heads and the leaves are extremely crisp. It's versatile too, for it can be sown in both the spring and autumn (Picture: Ian and Stuart Unwin)

Potatoes – is it worth saving your own seed?

Many people have grown a fair crop of potatoes from their own seed saved from the previous season. They may ask if we are not being kidded with false scares into buying expensive Scotch and Irish seed when their own would have done just as well.

The answer is – not completely. There are dangers in potato-seed saving. Things can go wrong and there are just as many failures as successes; no one boasts about those, of course.

The risk, however, is worth taking in years when potatoes are scarce. As the failures can generally be traced to mistakes in the way the seed was selected and saved, it pays to take great care with these operations.

Tubers must not be taken indiscriminately from any potato crop, or worse still from any bagful bought for eating from a shop or supermarket. This is asking for trouble, and it very often comes.

Select them from a good healthy crop that you have seen grow, and keep them properly during the time they are out of the ground; then they may well give a crop better than the original.

What are the hidden dangers and what must be looked out for? First it must be said that although we call them seed, these selected tubers are not, of course, seed at all. If they were, we should not have so much trouble, because diseases are rarely passed on in seed.

The seeds of potatoes are in those little tomato-like fruits that sometimes follow the flowers – but that's another story. Each tuber is part of the one it grew from and will have the same diseases, and if you save ten tubers from a diseased plant, you have ten diseased plants next year.

Because of the way we propagate potatoes, disease can spread like lightning, and with such an important crop – the most important in the country – it could be disastrous.

Viruses are the main trouble. They are microscopic organisms in the sap of plants and the two that most affect potatoes are leaf roll and mosaic. They are spread from plant by greenfly, which, after being on a diseased plant, carry it to every other plant they land on. The virus multiplies and is carried in the sap to every part of the plant, infecting every tuber it produces and guaranteeing diseased plants if these tubers are planted next year.

We are never as worried about greenfly on potatoes as we are on roses, for instance, and consequently the average gardener never sprays them with insecticide. Commercial crops are always sprayed, and those intended particularly for seed are grown where greenfly are not prolific. Hence Scotch and Irish seed, produced in isolated and 'clean' districts.

Leaf roll is the most troublesome and common of the potato viruses. The leaves roll upwards and inwards to a kind of tube, and they may also have a purple tinge to their margins. Growth is sometimes stiff and stunted with the leaves pointing upright, rather than horizontally and, late in the season, they turn brown and dry up.

It is not easy to distinguish some of these symptoms in a year when drought has affected all growth. But if there is any doubt at all, the advice must be – don't risk it.

Mosaic affects different varieties in different ways. In Majestic, brown streaks run along the vines on the undersides of the leaves. On King Edward and Home Guard it's in the form of brown spots which turn yellow and shrivel, with the leaflets hanging on by a thread.

In Arran Pilot and Ulster Chieftan, a yellow mottling is the only sign. There is a general dwarfing, though again this is difficult to recognise in a dry year, and the stems hardly seem strong enough to hold themselves upright. Tubers from mosaic-affected plants are always small.

Pentland Crown is resistant to both these viruses. Desirée, Ulster Chieftain and Pentland Beauty are resistant to mosaic, but only moderately resistant to leaf roll.

If certified seed is bought, it means that the crop was inspected while growing by Department of Agriculture inspectors and passed as 'clean'. Without this inspection there is always a risk, but it is worth taking in these times as long as the symptoms above are kept in mind.

Common scab on potatoes is a disease that is not necessarily passed on. It is best not to keep badly affected tubers, but the odd few marks can be ignored; they will not affect next year's crop.

One other important precaution. When selecting seed, don't dig up a row or rows and then go along picking up all the tubers of seed size. You may well by this method be picking up the biggest tubers from the poorest roots.

Rather select as you dig, saving all the tubers – except the very small – from particularly good roots. This way, you are sure of propagating from only the best.

Sensible cloching

Cloches can be just as useful in the autumn as in the spring, and it's a pity for them to be lying idle when they could be protecting plants against frost and bad weather.

But don't be over-enthusiastic with them. They won't work miracles and there are some things that can be actually damaged by cloching too soon.

Strawberries, for instance. Because you can get earlier fruit from under cloches, there's a temptation to think that the earlier you put them on, the earlier you'll be picking. This is wrong. The time to cloche strawberries is around late February.

If they're put on now, soft growth may well be induced before Christmas and this will almost surely be cut down by hard frosts in January. Far from gaining anything, a lot may be lost.

The danger is just the same with winter greenstuff. It might seem to the beginner that protection would be a good thing for, say, January King cabbage or winter cauliflowers.

Don't be tempted. They are quite hardy if left to grow normally. But try to coddle them now, and the soft growth they make will inevitably be damaged when the weather is at its worst.

The same applies to the spring-cabbage plants we shall be setting out at any time now.

Again they are quite hardy, and if you want to cut them as spring greens rather than leave them to heart up, a cloche in February will push the valuable new growth on. A cloche now will do nothing.

The decision about what to cover in the autumn and what is better left until spring can be made by looking at when the crop is expected to mature.

The things to cloche in the next few weeks are those that are needed to hang on late from this season.

The ones to cloche in the late winter and early spring are those that are to be pushed on for next season.

For instance, late sowings of summer lettuce that are liable to be damaged by the first frost or too much wet, can be kept going, perhaps until Christmas, by covering at the first signs of deterioration in the weather, generally sometime in late September and October.

But hardy winter lettuce such as Arctic King are better left uncovered until severe frosts threaten, perhaps as late as January or February.

Late sowings made this year of carrots or beetroot, or onions put in for pulling for Christmas salads, will appreciate a bit of cover, and spinach or even late-sown peas can give late and very welcome pickings if covered before the rot sets in. So, too, can French beans.

But autumn-sown onions intended for pulling or transplanting next spring, or broad beans sown in November, are best left uncovered at least until the turn of the year.

The other excellent use for cloches at this time of the year is as an aid to finishing off the ripening of crops.

Outdoor tomatoes will go on ripening well if all the leaves are stripped off and the plants laid down and covered.

If straw is put down underneath them and the cloche ends covered, the small fruits will go on swelling for a few more weeks rather than stopping and perhaps shrivelling up, as they do when picked before they are mature.

Onions can often be dried off with cloches over them, as can shallots. And in years when it is difficult to get carrots or beetroot dry for putting into store, the same applies.

A word of warning though: this must not be tried with potatoes. If they are exposed to light for more than a few hours they will turn green and become uneatable.

Digging maincrop potatoes

Once the haulm of maincrop potatoes begins to die down, there is no point in leaving them in the ground. Here they are subject to secondary growth and to the ravages of soil pests, so the sooner they are lifted the better.

1 Lift carefully, using a fork and working from the side of the row. Any potatoes that are speared with the fork should be used immediately and not stored.

2 Lay the tubers out on the ground for a few hours before taking them in for storage.

3 Haulm can easily spread disease, so it is better to remove it and put it on the bonfire.

October

Get digging! Yes, it's time to get the spade out again. As crops are lifted, the veg plot should be cleared and dug over. And the sooner you do this the better. By digging now, the soil will be weathered and replenished throughout the winter. You may well only be able to do small areas at a time because some crops will still be in the ground, but do them you should. Leave it any later, and bad weather may set in, and you may not be able to get onto the plot to dig until the spring.

You'll find digging and clearing an established veg plot far easier than tackling a wild, virgin site, something you may have had to do when you first created your vegetable garden.

The crops you will be clearing this month should include runner beans, savoys, spinach, beetroot, turnips, kohl rabi and salsify.

Jobs for the month

In the greenhouse

Sow seeds of 'short-day' lettuce for planting in a warm greenhouse for winter cutting.

Outside

Lift carrots and beetroot and store in moist sand.

Dig all potatoes. Dry, and store in sacks in a dry frostproof place.

Store onions in nets.

Plant out spring cabbages and protect from slugs.

Earth up celery for the last time.

Place cloches over lettuce.

Pick and dry runner beans selected for seed.

Saving seed potatoes

Provided your potato crop is healthy, it is well worth while saving your own. Take seed only from healthy plants that have produced a good crop.

1 Select healthy-looking plants and dig up a few to find a good cropper from which to save the seed.

2 Allow these tubers to lie on the surface of the soil for a few days. A little greening will encourage sprouting later.

3 Save all but the smallest potatoes from the best plants, setting them on dry soil or peat in a box.

4 Cover the tubers again with dry soil or peat, and place the box in a cool, dry, frost-free shed.

Spring cabbage – last planting of the year

Spring cabbage are the last of the veg we put out this year. They can be planted at any time in October – even into November – but it is best to see them well established before the worst of the weather comes and early this month generally seems to be about the best time.

They will be usable next spring when there is little else about – March or May – so it might pay to put in an extra row or two. In these rows plant at half the usual distance, 9in (23cm) instead of 18in (50cm) so that an early start can be made with cutting.

The long cutting season is one of their main attributes. Close planting allows every alternate plant to be cut when it is still just 'spring greens', perhaps in February, while the others are left to go on growing, to be used continuously through March, April and May.

There shouldn't be any shortage of plants, but if you haven't grown your own or can't buy any, you can always buy seed. Though it's too late to sow them for transplanting later, a row could be sown thinly across the garden, and the seedlings thinned out, leaving those you want undisturbed at 9in (23cm) apart.

Slugs will be the main problem in this case, and they must be guarded against with pellets or slug liquid. Don't overdo spring-cabbage planting. Remember you can't autumn or winter dig where they stand, and this may interfere with your spring sowing and planting plans.

Frost protection

When the first frosts threaten, ripening crops must be protected or cleared and used if they are likely to be affected by low temperatures. Outdoor tomatoes can be ripened under cloches.

1 Spread a good thick layer of straw or peat around the base of the plants.

2 Carefully cut the plant away from its supporting cane.

3 Taking care not to damage the stem, lay the plant horizontally on the straw.

4 Cover with cloches. Remember to close the ends to prevent wind tunnelling through.

5 **Self-blanching celery is frost-tender, so it must be lifted and used.**

6 **Draw a little soil around the roots of celeriac to keep them white and tender.**

7 **The rain will start millions of weed seedlings into growth. Hoe them out while they're still small.**

All about manuring

The best thing for any vegetable garden in the next few weeks is the promise of a load of farmyard manure. The easiest and least complicated method of growing good crops next year is to dig in good farmyard muck, in almost any quantity, between now and Christmas. Without any other additions at all, except possibly lime on acid soils, any ground well manured in the autumn will grow veg to a very good standard.

This doesn't mean to say that water given at the right time while crops are growing won't add extra weight, or that extra food won't make a difference. Both most likely will. But basically, soil plus farmyard manure, plus lime if necessary, will grow almost anything without adding anything else.

If there is any chance of getting a load in your district – and this is sometimes the hardest part of the whole business – do so, as soon as ever you can. There's plenty of time yet to dig it in, so you have a few weeks to look around and even shop around if you have any choice of supplier.

If there is any choice, best of all for the job is cow manure and straw, and don't worry about it being too 'fresh'. The freshness will be gone out of it by the time it's in contact with next year's crops, whether it's dug in now or whether it's stacked and used in the spring.

Strong, fresh farmyard manure is dangerous only when it is used immediately on growing crops. Dig it in now, and its valuable 'fire' will go into the ground for the benefit of everything.

There is no bad manure. Horse manure is lighter and so more of it is needed to do the same job. Pig manure is strong, cold and acid, and needs a lot of bulky material with it, such as straw, leaves, peat or any other vegetable matter. Poultry manure is also strong, and again needs bulk with it.

They are all good for the garden. Use any of them you can get. Dig in whatever you can by Christmas, then stack the rest to use later.

Having said all this, don't despair if you can't get any of these top manures – there are plenty of good substitutes, and many gardeners rely on them entirely.

Available in many places in almost unlimited quantities is used mushroom compost. This is partly animal manure, but so much decomposed that its fertilising and feeding value has dropped almost to nil. It is about on the same level as leaves or peat or garden compost. There's plenty of bulk in it, good for soil conditioning, excellent for holding water where roots can get at it, but low in minerals, the vital foods that plants must have.

This is where the artificial manures come in. With the soil made physically and mechanically good by the addition of bulk, whatever it is, a product such as Growmore is needed to add the vital spark.

Used in addition to generous farmyard manure, these proprietary fertilisers are something of a luxury, but with ordinary vegetable bulky matter they are almost a necessity.

The best way is to rake them into the surface, at the recommended quantity, a week or two before sowing or planting in the spring. What the mushroom compost, the leaves, the peat, or anything else are lacking, proprietary fertilisers will supply.

A product that goes a long way to supplying almost anything, and so begins to approach farmyard manure in general value, is the compost made by several municipal authorities, consisting of dried sewage mixed with pulverised dustbin rubbish.

Many thousands of tons of this are now being used both commercially and by amateurs. It is not unpleasant in any way, having the appearance and consistency of a mixture of soil and peat, and as it can be bought in handy polythene sacks it can conveniently be used anywhere.

Regard it as an in-betweener. Not quite as good as farmyard manure, but better in food value than the plain leaves, lawn mowings or garden compost. It can be used just as it is, or mixed with anything else, and it can be dug in or spread on top of the ground after digging.

One last word. It may seem early to be talking about manures for next year. But these materials are so vital and necessary for good gardening, that it is never too early to be making sure of your supply.

Transplanting winter lettuce

Winter lettuce should now be big enough to transplant. Thin the rows carefully, removing the transplants with a trowel. While summer lettuce will romp away if you just throw them in the soil, winter varieties are subject to all sorts of problems, so you must take much more care. Prepare the ground by raking in 3oz per sq yd (85gm per sq m) of bone meal.

1 Always handle seedlings by the leaves. Damage to the stems will almost certainly mean fungus diseases later.

2 If you have not sown a variety resistant to root aphis, the seedlings should be dipped in malathion before planting.

3 **In fine soil, the quickest way is to plant with your fingers, but you may prefer to use a trowel.**

4 **Firm in the roots well. Make sure that the soil is in contact with the roots right down at the bottom.**

Growing runner beans from tubers

Few people grow runner beans from tubers and there are plenty of gardeners who don't even know it can be done.

For them, then, let's put it on record that the runner-bean plant does make a tuber, very much like a dahlia, and as with a dahlia, the roots can be kept from one year to another and grown on.

They have to be dug up and stored in a frostproof place and the time to do it is now, because they won't live through the winter left in the ground.

However, it is not a particularly recommended method. Sometimes the tubers are lost by shrivelling in store. In any case a row of runner beans grown in the normal way from seed will usually do much better overall than a neighbouring row grown from tubers.

The one advantage of using tubers is that they will normally give you earlier beans. This is all that can be said, however. After their first, small flush, they don't compare with the seed row. Beans are easy enough to grow from seed, and there is not much point in saving the tubers.

If you still want to have a go, select some good plants, cut the tops off a few inches above ground level, dig them up carefully and shake off the surplus soil.

Then bury them in a box of slightly damp peat and keep them in a cool place, frostproof of

Runner beans make tuberous roots that can be kept from one year to another. But only use the tubers from good, healthy plants.

Seeds of different runner bean varieties are generally different colours. They can be black, white or speckled.

course, exactly as you would a dahlia tuber. Remember, though, that they can shrivel and die as well as freeze, so they will need watching and keeping slightly damp.

It's best to start them up in the spring in the greenhouse or cold frame, before planting them out. But don't whatever you do, fall into the trap of starting them growing too soon.

They can't be planted out until the middle of June, and if you start them too soon the several shoots that come from each tuber will get tangled in the most unholy mess: you'll lose everything you might have gained by damaging them in the unwinding. When they're in this mess, too, it's also difficult to get them to start climbing.

Keep them cold and dry until the beginning of May. Then the shoots will be only a few inches long by June, just right for planting out and getting away.

While talking about beans, if you've saved yourself some seeds, make sure they're bone-dry before you put them away. The best place for them after they've been shelled is laid out on a newspaper on the greenhouse staging for a week or two. Then put them in a bag or packet in a safe place.

Saving runner-bean seed

Many or your own seeds can be saved for next year, and none more successfully than runner beans. Don't save seed from any old plant – select those that have given the biggest crop of good-quality beans. This way, you will eventually improve the strain.

1 Remove the pods when they are dry and papery.

2 Put them in an airy, sunny spot to dry out completely.

3 When all the pods are quite dry, the seeds can be removed.

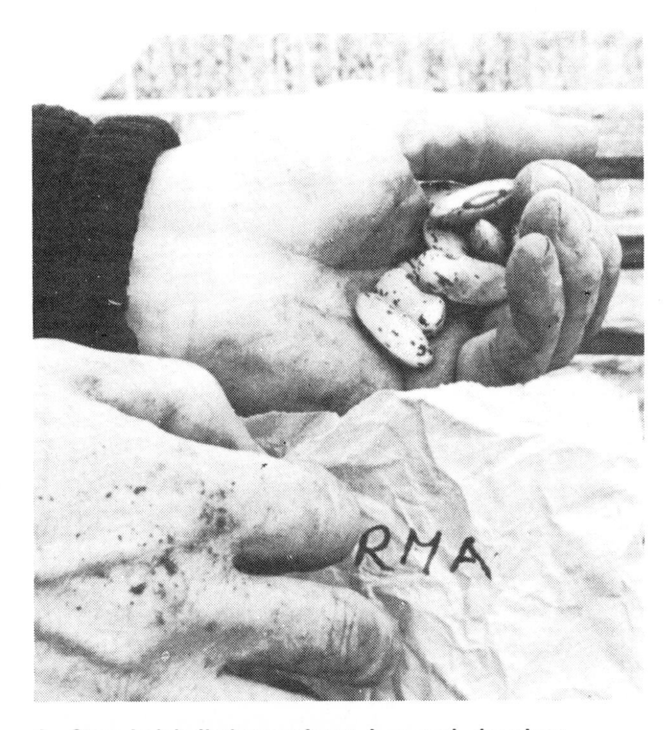

4 Store in labelled paper bags, in a cool, dry place.

Forcing chicory

It's a matter of opinion, but for some people, forced chicory is just about the best winter salad going. If you have grown it in the garden, roots can be forced throughout the winter from now on. If not, it is possible to buy roots for forcing at some garden centres.

1 Lift a few plants from the garden, taking care to avoid damage.

2 With a sharp knife, cut off the foliage just above the top of the root.

3 If the root is too long to fit your pots, the end can also be trimmed.

4 Put a little garden soil in a 9in (23cm) pot and set the roots in it.

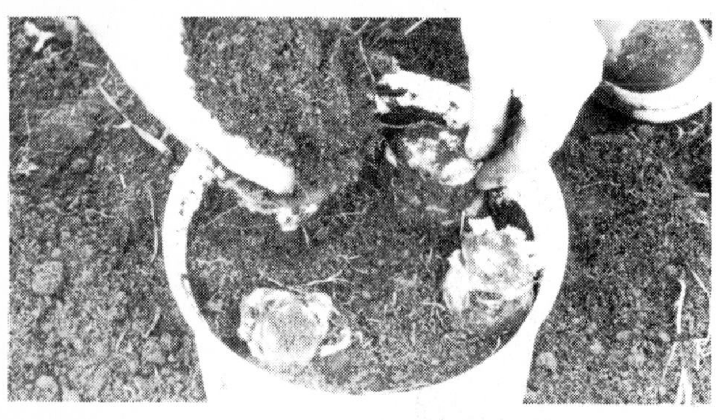

5 Surround the roots right up to the crowns with garden soil.

6 Take the pot into the greenhouse and cover with another pot.

7 It is essential to exclude all light, so cover the holes. You can use a small ball of clay.

Crisp chicory . . . some folk reckon it's the best winter salad going.

November

Manure! Remember to order it and get it dug into the ground if the weather permits. If not, leave the job until a bright, dry spell later in the winter or early spring.

The plot should still be producing plenty of vegetables, including brussels sprouts, celery, leeks and Jerusalem artichokes. Pick sprouts as soon as they are tight and firm, working from the bottom of the plant upwards. The best way to get them off the stems is with a sharp knife. Celery of the self-blanching type is not hardy, so watch for any signs of frost.

As for parsnips, the longer they can be left in the ground the better. Exposure to frost increases their sugar content so they have a better flavour later on. The way to harvest Jerusalem artichokes is to cut down and clear the stems in November, and then dig up the tubers like potatoes as and when you want them.

There is just one crop you can sow this month – broad beans. The advantage of sowing now is that you get an earlier crop next year. But make sure you sow an autumn variety and although they are quite hardy, it pays to play safe by covering with cloches to protect them against any really heavy frosts during the winter.

Jobs for the month

Outside

Sow broad beans in sheltered positions.

Use black cotton to protect spring-cabbage plants from birds.

Remove and gather up yellowing leaves of brussels sprouts.

Protect cauliflower curds from frost.

Dig parsnips and Jerusalem artichokes as required.

Order manure ready for winter digging.

Storing root crops

Swedes, turnips and beetroot should be lifted and stored now. If you have a large quantity they can be clampea outside, but make sure you have some in boxes of peat or soil in the shed as well. There's nothing worse than a trip down the garden to unclamp vegetables on cold winter evenings.

1 Lift the roots carefully with a fork. Avoid damaging or bruising them or they will not store well.

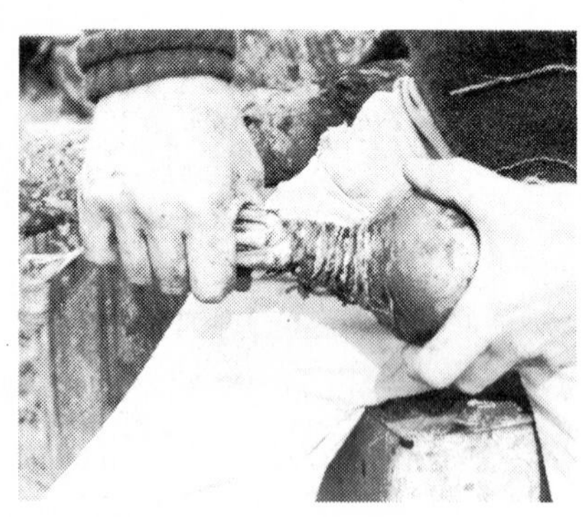

2 Twist off the foliage and put the leaves on the compost heap. They can be cut off, but make sure not to cut into the root.

3 Find a convenient corner of the garden and spread out a layer of clean straw about 6in (15cm) deep

4 Pile the roots on to the straw base in a cone-shaped heap and leave them for a day or two to 'sweat'.

Early digging

The vegetable gardeners who come off best in drought seasons – whatever their soil – are undoubtedly those who get their digging done in the autumn and winter.

Early digging is generally recommended so that we can be reasonably sure that the surface will work well at sowing and planting time. But, when a dry season follows, it has another great advantage: it is much slower to dry out.

When digging is left until the spring, there is an inescapable fact to be faced. It is that when ground is turned over, the naturual upward movement of moisture – known as capillary action – is checked for a time. If there is not enough rain to re-soak the top spit, movement is slow to start again, and the disturbed soil dries out, independently of the moisture lower down. This is what happens with late digging when a dry season follows.

Ground dug as late as March or April never really gets wet again and has little chance of producing a decent crop. Ground dug before Christmas will have at least some rain on it, allowing it to settle down and capillary action to re-start.

The best example of this complete drying out of newly dug soil is seen where it is dug for summer bedding plants. Where wallflowers, polyanthus, bulbs, etc, have to be removed, and the ground forked over, it dries out and stays dry all the season through.

Sowings and plantings of vegetables on ground that is dug following such late-moved crops as spring cabbage, leeks and parsnips, have much the same conditions to put up with, and so do plants following the early-dug potatoes.

The best crops, apart from those you can water well, come from early sowings made on ground that has been winter dug.

The lesson then is plain. Early digging pays. No one knows, of course, what sort of season we shall have. It may be dry, it may be wet. Only one thing is sure: if it's very dry, those who leave their digging the latest will suffer the worst.

Jerusalem artichokes

For women (or men, come to that) who are watching their weight, Jerusalem artichokes make an ideal alternative to potatoes because they contain no starch. They can be dug throughout the winter from now on.

1 Cut down the foliage of all the plants to prevent them blowing over during winter gales.

2 Dig the roots carefully, taking care not to damage the tubers.

4 Put a layer of peat in the bottom of a deep seed tray and lay the tubers on it.

3 Don't forget to save a few tubers for next year. Select healthy, round roots about 2in (5cm) long.

5 Cover the tubers with peat and store in a cool, dry, frost-free shed.

Celeriac

Celeriac can stand a little frost, but at this time of year it is safer to lift and store them. They store very well.

1 Lift the plants carefully to avoid damage, shaking as much soil as possible from the roots.

2 Cut off the foliage and put it on the compost heap. The fibrous roots can also be trimmed.

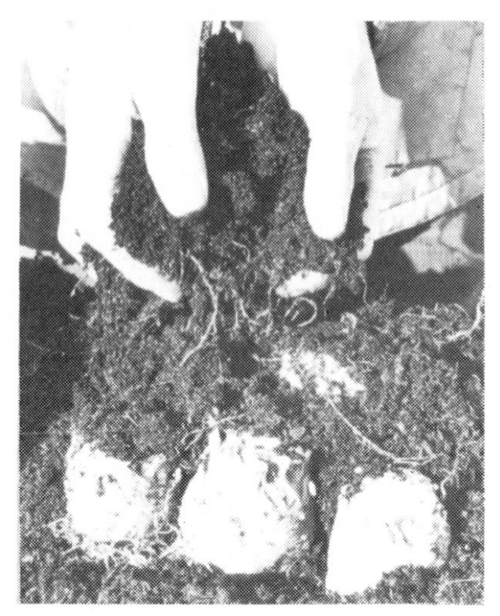

3 Put a little peat or sand into a box and lay the trimmed roots in it.

4 Cover with dry peat and sand, and store in an airy, frost-free shed.

December

Take it easy! Yes, this is the one month of the year when the vegetable gardener can sit back and put his feet up . . . assuming the important jobs such as manuring and digging have been done. If not, and the weather permits, drag on the woollies and get outside!

Do keep an eye on the weather and protect any crops in the ground if a really bad cold spell is forecast. Earth-up broad beans and spring cabbages by drawing a little soil around them, and cover other crops with straw. If you're storing produce in a shed, it's also wise to cover the trays or boxes with straw. You can never be too careful.

If you have time to put your feet up, spend a moment or two reviewing your successes and failures on the veg plot during the past year, and promise yourself you won't make the same mistakes next year (assuming, of course, you did go wrong somewhere along the line).

It's never too early to plan your veg plot for next year – working out which crops you will want to grow and preparing a rotation plan.

Jobs for the month

In the greenhouse

Be sure heating apparatus is in order for an early start next month.

Outside

Wheel manure on to vacant ground when frosty.

Dig whenever possible.

Examine all vegetables in store and remove any diseased.

Send for seed catalogues.

Apply slug killer round lettuce and spring cabbage plants.

Early sowings

The veg seeds we sow in heat early in the year to get super early crops are divided into two distinct sections – and it's a distinction that it's important to know about.

Into the first group go tomatoes, cucumbers, aubergines and peppers. Into the second go lettuce, cauliflower, cabbage, brussels sprouts, leeks and onions.

Perhaps you can see the significant difference. The first group are all things that must have warmth, not only to get them started but also to keep them going, at least until the middle of April and possibly on into May. The second lot only need warmth to get them started and for a week or two after. In fact they can be out in a cold frame by the end of February, just covered with glass or polythene.

Vegetables in the first group sown in mid-January will need heat for perhaps four months; those in the second group can manage with heat for only four or perhaps five weeks.

There's a difference in the amount of heat they need too. Tomatoes, etc, must have 65°F (18°C) to get them through, then never falling below 55°F (13°C) the whole time. The lettuce group need only 55°F (13°C) to start them, dropping to 45°F (7°C) when they are nicely away, and then, quite quickly, to no heat at all. Quite a difference this, when you come to reckon up how much these early crops are going to cost to keep warm.

To gain the full advantage from an early start, the varieties used must be quick maturing. 'Hispi' cabbage is one of the fastest growing of all. A kitchen windowsill can be used to start seeds, but it presents problems when the seedlings have to be pricked out or potted on. Some vegetables can be started this way and then moved out into a cold frame after two or three weeks.

It's a difference too, that makes it possible for only those with warm greenhouses to be successful with the first group, but for almost anyone to grow the second. For these, all that is needed is a not-too-cold windowsill in a living-room, and a cold frame outside. If you can manage this, and fancy having a go, here are a few points.

First, if it's going to be worth doing at all, it's worth doing it right.

Don't, for instance, 'spoil the ship for a ha-porth of tar' by trying to make do with any old soil or compost to sow your seeds in. The best bet, without any doubt, for seed sowing, and particularly as early as this, is one of the no-soil composts such as Levington. It doesn't take much to start a few pots or pans and it can be bought in quite small amounts in polythene bags from garden centres or supermarkets.

Second, to gain the maximum benefit from an early start, you must have real early varieties. Webbs Wonderful lettuce, for instance, might be your favourite for outside in the garden, but magnificent lettuce as it undoubtedly is, there are varieties that will grow much more quickly. They may not have all Webbs Wonderful's famous attributes, but earliness is what we're after in this particular exercise, so the quick-growing varieties are best. Among them are such as Fortune, Tom Thumb and May King.

The same goes for cabbage and cauliflowers. It would be a waste of time, for instance, sowing Winningstadt cabbage in January, however much you like it, or Canberra cauliflowers, because this would only make them mature in midsummer instead of their natural time in autumn. We are looking for something to cut in June or even earlier, so must use the Snowball types of cauliflower and quick-maturing cabbage like Hispi or Greyhound.

Third, even with this second group, if your facilities are limited to a warm living-room and a cold frame, don't be too ambitious. Remember that the seedlings will be through in three or four days, and unless you have big and light windowsills, they will have to be out in the cold frame a week or so after that – and it could still be very cold indeed.

Don't sow too early. Not before the middle of January. Towards the end would be better.

Brassicas – seeds or plants?

With the seed order still in mind, let's look at the pros and cons of either growing your own cabbages, etc, from seed and producing your own plants, or of relying on buying plants that someone else has grown.

In either case, unless you're lucky, they are going to cost you money. However, if you're hoping to grow a full quota of early and late cabbages and cauliflowers, calabrese, brussels, and heading and purple-sprouting broccoli, it will pay to buy seeds and grow your own.

Better still, if you can manage it, go shares with someone and buy seeds between you. You'll find that even the smallest packets will produce enough plants for two or three average gardens.

There are extra benefits too, in buying seeds. Almost the only way you can obtain plants of some tomato varieties is to buy seeds and grow your own. It's even more so with the greenstuff family.

A cabbage plant, of whatever variety, is just a cabbage plant to a lot of people who sell them, and worse still, that so-called cabbage may turn out to be a brussels sprout. Similarly, a cauliflower you are expecting to be ready in July, might be a broccoli that won't be cuttable until June the following year. These things have happened many times.

The trouble is the plants all look alike at planting time. Even the experts can't tell a late savoy from an early one at that stage, or an early cauliflower from late.

Now the people who packet the seeds don't make these mistakes. If it says Hispi or Winningstadt on the packet, you can be sure that's what is inside. And when you think that Hispi hearts up in June and Winningstadt in October, you can see how important this is.

The other point with greens is that we tend to treat all brassica plants with a little too much scorn. Given a drop of water, they recover very easily when they are planted, however poor and stricken they look, and we tend to think they don't mind rough handling, or having their roots and leaves shrivelled up in a drying wind or hot sunshine on a market stall.

In fact it's sometimes said that a check like this does them good, and some people purposely leave spring-cabbage plants out to wither before planting them. This is hard to believe.

The one benefit above all the others of having your own seed-bed is that you can carefully lift plants – note lift them, not drag them out in handfuls – and transplant them quickly and carefully, just as we do with some precious bedding plant that we have raised.

Surely a plant grown and moved with as little check as possible is better than one that has been half-dead out of the ground for a week. It's a certainty that the reason for a lot of failures, with cauliflowers especially, is a check of any kind.

When a plant thinks it is dying, it naturally tries to produce its flower and seed and, as cauliflowers are bred purposely to do this anyway, the slightest check will start them on their way. Then we get 'buttoning' as it's called – small, premature heads of hardly any use at all. A bad period at planting time accounts for a lot of this trouble.

The same goes for brussels sprouts. If they quickly get away after planting, they are bound to make a bigger and more productive plant.

Many growers, far from rough-handling their brassica plants, transplant them twice: once from the seed-bed into positions a couple of inches or so apart – a sort of nursery bed – and finally into their permanent places. This builds up a big root system, and growth never stops. It's a far cry from begging or buying wizened plants that may have been out of the ground for a week or two.

It's a little more trouble, sowing seeds and nursing them on to transplanting size, and of course they take up a bit of room in the garden, but it's only for a short time; in the end it's well worth it.

Winter lettuce under cloches

Early fresh salad crops are always expensive to buy, so it's a good idea to plant out some winter hardy lettuces under cloches on any workable piece of well-drained soil.

1 Fork over ground cleared of crops and remove any weeds, then rake level after breaking down the soil into a fine tilth. Remember, lettuces like a well-drained soil containing plenty of organic material.

2 Transplant October-sown varieties, taking care not to damage the delicate root systems, spacing them about 9in (23cm) each way. Take care not to bury the neck of the seedlings.

3 Early lettuces will need the protection of cloches in the open ground. Position self-watering cloches so that drips will not fall onto plants – often a common cause of loss.

4 Secure end-pieces to prevent draughts and stop the ravages of hungry birds. Keep a sharp look out for aphids during mild spells and control these with an insecticidal dust.

Turning on the heat

Suddenly it's almost seed-sowing time again. Not for everybody, of course, but for those with warmth enough in a greenhouse it's at least time to be thinking of the earliest sowings and buying the seeds.

First though, of course, you must decide whether early sowings are worth the heat they take. The question of the cost looms high, because to gain the full benefit an early start does mean providing heat by around the middle of January.

This doesn't mean you have to heat the whole house at that time. The few pots and pans needed for the first seeds take up only a small space, and quite a small, electrically-heated propagator, a soil-warming cable set in an area of sand, or the more recently developed heated staging, will easily accommodate them until it's time to prick them out or pot them on. And that might be five or six weeks – quite a saving. As these take little electricity anyway, the initial outlay for them is well worthwhile.

The same thing can be done with a small paraffin heater set underneath a small area of staging. It's even possible at least to get the seeds started, and just through the surface, in a warm living-room, as long as it is recognised – and here's the rub – that immediately they are through, they will need the full light of the greenhouse. A windowsill is just not good enough. Even this in-the-home exercise will save a week or so's heating.

So the big question must be: 'What is there to be gained by these early sowings?' Well, let's take the crops one at a time. First, tomatoes. It's quite easy, if you're determined enough, to buy tomato plants around the middle of March, which is about the time your own January-sown seeds will be ready. These will be plants someone else has grown, all ready to set out in the fruiting places.

What isn't so easy is to obtain at that time the variety you may want. It's all very well reading, or being told, about the great qualities of Sonata, Maas Cross, Alicante or the brand-new F1 hybrid varieties, but it's a different thing going out and trying to buy these as plants.

Often there's little choice, perhaps no choice at all. Yet it's no trouble to get almost any variety you fancy as a packet of seeds.

Add to that the fact that when you grow your own, your plants will be there on the job just when you want them, no waiting for delivery or having to fetch them, and these two things alone make the whole exercise worthwhile.

Of course the more things you can start in that small heated spot, the more economical it will be. As with the tomatoes, you can always buy a bit later in the year ready-to-set-out plants of lettuce, early brussels, cabbage and cauliflower, peppers and aubergines and cucumbers if you want to grow them, and onions and leeks if you fancy growing big ones. But you can't always drop on them the day you want them, and again they're not always of the varieties you particularly want.

So, even if you feel that early tomatoes are beyond you, and will take a bit too much heat (because, of course, they need some warmth for a long time after they're just seedlings, and so incidentally do cucumbers, aubergines and peppers), the lettuce, early greenstuff, leeks and onions don't. Almost as soon as they're pricked out, they can go straight into a cold house or a cold frame to harden off ready for planting outside in March.

Early vegetables are a must for the keen gardener. Even though an early start is going to cost money, taking all things into consideration, and being careful to do it the right way, they can still be made to pay.

Fruit

Choosing

When deciding which fruits to grow in your garden, there is one golden rule. If you have a small garden, think small. Big trees and bushes can literally take over a small plot.

So, in the small garden, go only for those fruits with a compact habit. This doesn't mean you have to restrict yourself to soft fruits. There are several apples and pears (some of them normally thought of as fairly large trees) which crop really well when grown in pots or tubs; indeed they make attractive features on patios and paths.

Among the apples that can be grown in this way are Sunset, Ellison's Orange, Claygate Permain, May Queen and Lady Sudeley. The best pears for this type of growing are Louise Bonne, Conference, Laxton's Superb and Gorham.

In small gardens, apples and pears can also be grown as cordons. These take up very little room when, for example, they are planted alongside a path. Dwarf pyramid apple trees, which grow to a height of 3ft (1m), are also ideal.

And there is a further way of growing pears in the small garden – trained against a house wall in espalier form.

But when buying apple and pear trees (whether to grow as 'miniatures' or as full trees) pollination is an important point to bear in mind and it will probably mean that you have to buy more than one variety. To ensure heavy cropping, you must grow varieties that are compatible when it comes to pollination.

For example, the apple Cox's Orange Pippin will not set its own pollen. So if you buy this variety, you will also need other varieties such as Worcester Permain or Stirling Castle to ensure pollination.

The other popular tree fruits are peaches, cherries and plums. Recommended varieties of peaches are Barrington, Duke of York, Early Rivers, Hale's Early and Peregrine.

As for cherries, top of the list is Amber Heart, which is a really reliable cropper. Other recommended varieties include Bigarreau Napoleon, Bradbourne Black, Knight's Early Black, Merton Heart and Waterloo. But, as with apples and pears, proper pollination of cherries can be difficult.

Recommended varieties of plums (which can also be grown fan-shaped against a south or west wall in the small garden) are Czar, Laxton's Delicious, Thames Cross and, of course, Victoria. Some plums are self-fertile and will set fruit with their own pollen, but crops will be heavier if another variety is grown as a pollinator.

Finally, here are some recommended varieties of soft fruit.

Raspberries
Malling Jewel, Pyne's Royal, Glen Clova, Malling Admiral, Delight, Zeva, Golden Everest, Fallgold and November Abundance.

Blackberries
Bedford Giant, Merton Early, Ashton Cross, Himalaya Giant and Oregon Thornless.

Blackcurrants
Laxton's Giant, Mendip Cross, Wellington xxx, Tenah, Blacksmith, Westwick Triumph, Amos Black, Cotswold Cross and Blackdown.

Redcurrants
Fay's Prolific, Jonkheer Van Tets, Laxton's No 1, Houghton Castle, Red Lake, Wilson's Long Bunch and Rondom.

Gooseberries
Bedford Red, Broom Girl, Langley Gage, May Duke, Whitesmith, Bedford Yellow, Careless, Green Overall, Gunner, Laxton's Amber, Thumper, Howard's Lancer, Rifleman, White Lion and White Transparent.

Strawberries
Cambridge Premier, Cambridge Regent, Native de Caen, Cambridge Favourite, Cambridge Vigour, Domanil, Tamella, Cambridge Sentry, Royal Sovereign, Souvenir de Charles Machiroex, Cambridge Late Pine, Rabunda, Talisman, Montrose, Gento, La Sans Rivale, St Claude and Grandee.

Planting

Planting fruit trees, bushes and canes is one of the most important operations. When, and how it is done can influence the plant's performance throughout its life.

The best time for planting is early autumn, but they can also be planted throughout the winter months and early spring. Where late spring planting is necessary because of late deliveries, unsuitable soil conditions because of poor weather or a move to a new garden, it can be successful if some extra care is taken.

Water regularly to ensure that the plant has sufficient at all times, spray the trees and bushes with water once or twice a day if the weather is dry and warm, and during periods of cold drying winds, protect with polythene or hessian to reduce drying out of the wood.

Late-planted trained trees against sunny walls or fences usually suffer most, and as they are the most expensive, the extra attention is well worthwhile to get them away to a good start.

The soil on the planting sites should have been prepared well in advance. In the small garden, it is a sound policy to cultivate the whole area that is to be allocated to fruit to the depth of 18–20in (46–50cm). If the area has not been cultivated, individual stations will have to be prepared.

For top fruits (apples, pears, plums, peaches, etc) take out a hole 3ft (1m) in diameter. First, remove the top 10in (25cm) of soil, then dig over the lower spit as deep as possible, breaking the soil up and adding some bulky organic material. Now replace the top soil, adding and mixing well-decayed organic matter such as farmyard manure, peat or garden compost, plus 2oz (60gm) of superphosphate and 1oz (30gm) of sulphate of potash.

For bush fruits (black, red and white currants, and gooseberries) the stations can be slightly smaller. The site for cordon apples, pears, redcurrants, gooseberries and for raspberries will be an area not less than 3ft (1m) wide, thoroughly cultivated two spits deep along the whole length of the row.

Planting distances are always given with a certain amount of variation, which often leaves the beginner wondering which figure to use. For example, bush apples 10–15ft (3–4.5m) apart, fan trained trees 12–18ft (3.5–5.5m) apart, and so on.

The reason for this is that there are a number of factors that influence the growth of the trees. First, the cultivar itself. Some are known for vigorous growth, Bramley's Seedling, for instance, while Cox's Orange Pippin is of moderate to weak growth, according to the locality.

The rootstock on to which the cultivar has been budded has the greatest control over the ultimate size of the tree. The soil into which the tree is planted also has an effect on its size and vigour. The amount of rainfall plays a part, as, lastly, does your management of the trees – pruning, feeding and so on.

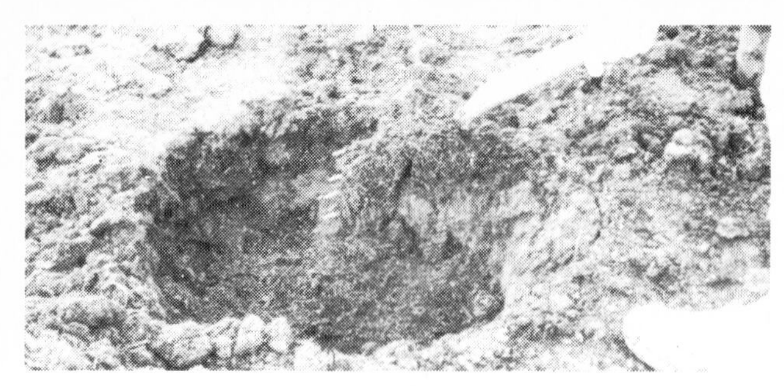

1 Individual stations should be prepared 3ft (90cm) in diameter, and after digging and manuring the bottom spit, peat or well-decayed organic matter is added to the top soil.

2 Any damaged roots are cut off cleanly to avoid rotting.

3 It is important to plant at the correct depth. A plank across the hole helps to show that the union where the tree was budded will be above the final soil level.

4 Firm and systematic treading of the soil as it is re-placed is essential—be careful, though, to avoid damaging the roots.

So apples planted as cordons at an angle of about 45 degrees should be 2ft (60cm) apart, and 6ft (2m) between rows, while pears as cordons require a little more space - 3ft (1m) between the trees. Bush apples on Malling No 9 and No 26 rootstocks, both of which are suitable for the small garden, can be spaced at 8–12ft (2.5–3.5m) apart, depending on the soil type, and whether it is a weak or strong growing cultivatar. Bush pears should be given the wider spacing on all soils.

Wall-trained trees of cherries, pears, plums, gages and peaches should never be allocated less than 10ft (3m) even in good soils, and cherries, plums and pears will need all 18ft (5.5m) if soil and growing conditions are poor. Trained trees are difficult enough to manage, even given sufficient space, but in small areas restrictive pruning soon leads to poor crops and other problems.

Blackcurrants will grow and crop well when planted close together - ie, at 3ft (1m) apart - but for garden planting 5ft (1.5m) between bushes is necessary. However, 4ft × 5ft (1.2m × 1.5m) is a good average spacing that can be used for black, red and white currants and gooseberries grown as bushes. The latter three can be grown as cordons, when 20in (50cm) apart is sufficient, or 30in (75cm) if they are trained as double cordons.

Raspberries are often planted too closely: 18in (45cm) should be allowed between the canes at planting time and as the root system develops the spaces will be filled. When growing conditions are good 6ft (1.8m) is needed between the rows, though 5ft (1.5m) is sufficient for the weaker-growing cultivars such as Lloyd George and Glen Clova.

Blackberries and loganberries trained on walls, fences or wire supports require 10–12ft (3–3.5m) per plant.

Trees and bushes should be unpacked as soon as possible after delivery from the nursery. The roots should never be left exposed to dry out, and if at all dry they should be sprayed, or better still soaked in water, before being placed in a trench with roots well covered with soil until they can be planted in the permanent positions.

When you begin planting, first take out a hole large enough for the roots of your tree or bush to spread out evenly. While this is being done, keep the roots of all other plants covered to prevent drying out.

Inspect the root system, prune cleanly all broken and damaged roots. Any very long main roots can be shortened.

The depth of planting is important, whatever the subject, but with top fruit the union between the rootstock and the cultivar must be kept well above the soil level. The general rule is to plant to the same depth as the nursery did: the soil line will indicate this quite clearly.

The one exception to this rule is the blackcurrant which should always be planted at least 4in (10cm) deeper, so that the base of the lower branches is below the soil.

Once the roots have been pruned and the depth of the hole adjusted to get the correct planting position, the roots can be covered with good, friable soil taken from the hole. Jerk the tree up and down a few times as the filling proceeds to ensure that the soil comes into close contact with the roots.

If soil conditions are bad and no friable soil is available, then a little prepared soil should be used to work among the roots.

The soil should be firmed by treading as the work of filling goes on as all fruit trees and bushes must be planted firmly. Loose planting is the cause of many failures and if when you have finished you can pull the tree up easily with one hand – well, start all over again!

Stakes will be required for bush, half-standard and standard apples, pears and plums. Round wooden stakes, not less than 2in (5cm) in diameter at the top and treated with a wood preservative, are ideal. For the standards they will need to be 8ft (2.5m) long; for the half-standards over 6ft (2m) long.

It's a good idea to drive the stake into position before planting the tree. This avoids damaging the root system and the branches. The ties should be placed in position but not finally tightened until after the trees have settled, for if planting has been carried out on newly-prepared ground, it may sink several inches and the tree must be able to settle with it.

Fruit and veg – the best of both worlds

It's a sad fact that when the average gardener thinks about growing his own produce, fruit tends to come second to vegetables.

Lack of room is the usual reason given and, where a particularly favourite fruit crop is planted, it's often relegated to the poorest site in the vegetable plot, or ends up in a narrow bed squeezed between a path and boundary fence (although this position may be used productively, if the right fruit is chosen).

There is no reason why you shouldn't sample the best of both worlds by creating a proper combined fruit/veg garden.

If you want the best results, you should plan the fruit and vegetable garden thoroughly before getting down to the digging and planting. Haphazard planting without regard to the size, the space available and the choice of varieties (most important for fruit) will only result in poor cropping and create undue work later.

So make a sketch of the area to be used and work out on paper just what and where vegetable and fruit crops will fit in to best advantage.

To help you with this puzzle, use as a guide the small family fruit and vegetable garden designed and recently planted up at the Royal Horticultural Society's garden at Wisley in Surrey. It is an ideal productive plot for an average garden and takes up an area of 40ft × 30ft (slightly more than 12m × 9m) including the pathways (see page 130).

If the shape of your garden prevents you using the design as it stands, break it down into the individual beds and site them in the most convenient positions your garden will allow.

Ideally, the fruit and vegetable plots are best placed together, where they can be screened off from the ornamental garden and the view from the house by a hedge of espalier or cordon fruit.

Alternatively, you can use an ornamental shrub, choosing for preference a plant that produces plenty of flowers: this will help to attract pollinating insects to the area – an important factor for most fruit and many vegetables. In the garden design, the espalier screen faces south towards the ornamental garden and house.

For preference, the site should face south for maximum light, and out of any deep shade cast by buildings or tall trees. Remember that planting under trees will increase the chances of damage from drips of water and the sticky, smothering honeydew given off by many insects.

Fruit varieties that flower early will need pro-

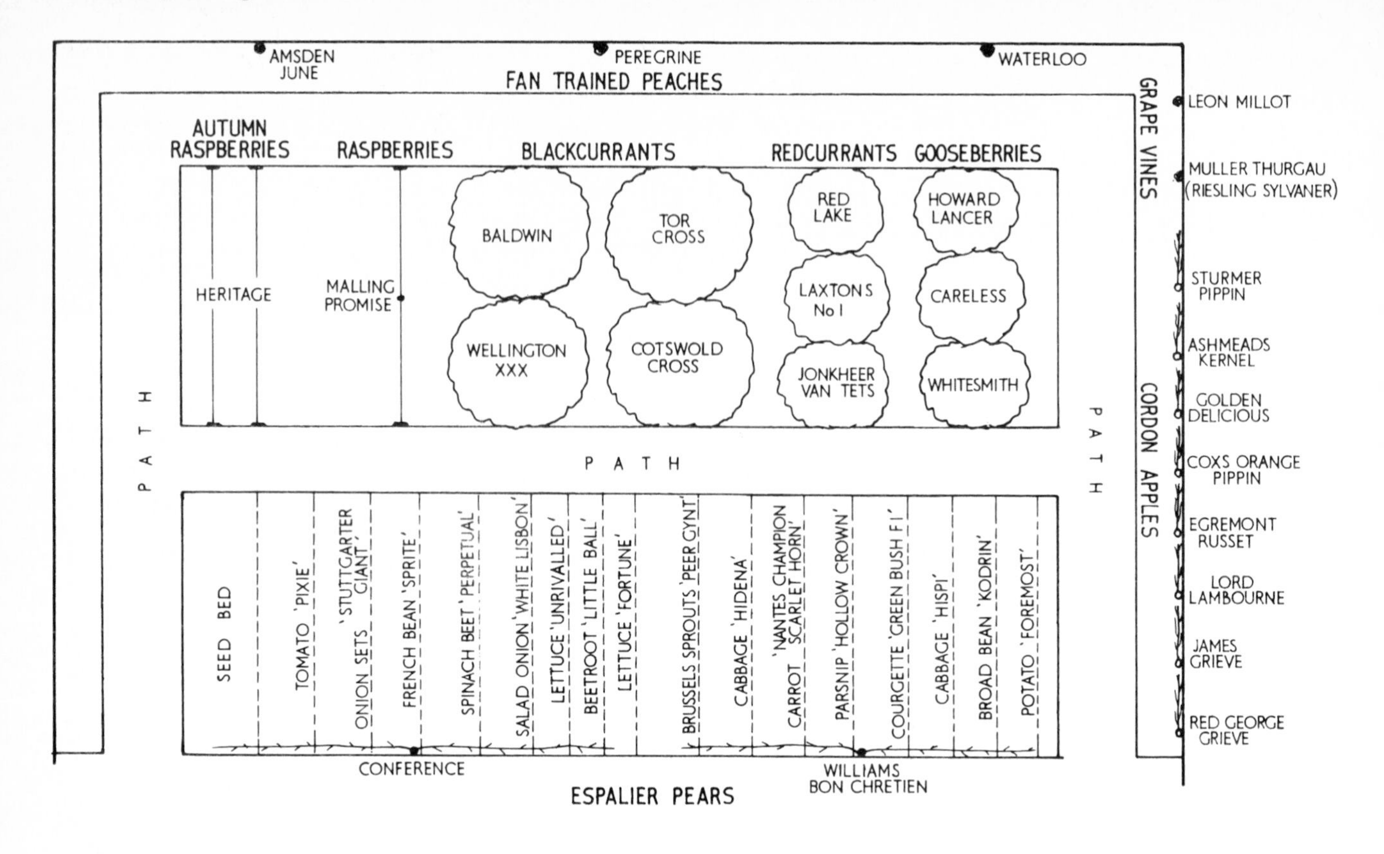

tection from cold winds and frost pockets. Hollows at the bottom of slopes should be avoided if possible.

If your garden is situated in a frost pocket, go for later-flowering fruit varieties. Screens and hedges of tall thick shrubs and trees will often trap cold air running down a slope, so it might be advisable to thin these out to allow a free air-flow away from the plot.

The opposite may be the case if your garden is exposed to cold winter winds; here it may be necessary to erect shelter in the form of fences. Choose open types like netting in particularly windy spots to help avoid turbulence damage on the leeward side.

Try to position the vegetable garden where it will not be overshadowed by the taller fruit bushes. And, if your boundary lines are marked by hedges, remember the vegetables and fruit will be competing with them for water and plant foods, so allow plenty of room between.

About 6ft (say 2m) would be ideal, but in restricted gardens, where space is at a premium, allow no less than 3ft (90cm) and give the crop extra feeding and water to compensate.

Good access is necessary if you're to work in comfort, so make allowances for paths in your design. Hard-surface paths are relatively maintenance-free and better to walk on during the wetter months of the year. However, grass is easier on the eye and may be preferred in informal gardens. Individual fruit trees can, of course, be planted in small pockets cut out of the turf if required.

The design is divided up into two main beds: a vegetable plot 30ft × 11ft (9.2m × 3.3m), soft cane and bush fruit in a bed 30ft × 12ft (9.2m × 3.6m) and a 2ft (60cm) wide boundary bed on three sides of the whole garden.

Not everyone will want exactly the same varieties given in the plan, but there's no reason why alternatives cannot be used, provided they are of similar form. The espalier pears, for instance, could be dropped in favour of espalier apples, or perhaps blackberries or loganberries trained on support wires.

In the narrow border on the left, the choice is yours, perhaps filling the stone-fruit gap by planting fan-trained morello cherries, plums or gages. Three plants could comfortably be incorporated in this space. Alternatively, you may prefer vegetables of a perennial nature, or even a selection of herbs.

This border would also provide seasonal vegetables such as runner beans, marrows (trained up tripods), or ridge cucumbers on supports.

In larger plots, half-standard plums and gages could be incorporated, as well as dwarf pyramid apples and pears. But when planning for larger trees, make sure they will not overshadow lower-growing crops.

Aim to group fruits of the same type together and never try to squeeze in extra plants in the hope you'll get higher yields from the same area. This does not work and lower, poor-quality yields will usually result.

Individual plants are shown on the plan, except for the raspberries, of which ten plants of each variety are required to make the 12ft (3.5m) rows.

Planting trees

Provided the ground is workable, most fruit bushes can be planted from containers at almost any time of the year you can get them.

Lifted stock from nursery beds is, however, best planted from leaf-fall until just before bud-burst, normally from October until early April, depending on the type and time of flowering.

Generally, soft fruits and restricted forms of top fruit are planted into beds that have been carefully dug and manured overall, but standard fruit trees are often planted into individual pockets, taken out of roughly dug or grassed areas.

Wherever possible, it pays to take out the planting holes in advance, as the heaps of infill soil can then be covered to stop them becoming saturated.

It also prevents delay if planting holes and infill soil can be covered as a protection against freezing – there's nothing worse than having the trees and not being able to get them in.

When your plants arrive, the immediate job is to unwrap them and check they're in good condition. If they're damaged, contact the suppliers promptly, otherwise you may find that they cannot be replaced without further charge.

Try to get them planted as soon as possible, but if soil or weather conditions are bad, they can be either heeled into a trench or stood in a protected place and covered with loose peat or damp sacking to prevent bare-rooted stock drying out.

If the stock is container grown, prevent the root-ball freezing solid in hard weather by covering with dry sacking or similar. Storing the plants in a frost-free shed is probably the ideal solution, but don't let the compost become dust-dry.

Another important item to remember when planting fruit crops is firm support, in the form of wire framework or stakes, so make sure you have the necessary materials at hand before planting begins.

Top fruits like apples and pears will need staking for a year or two until the trees become established and the supports should be sturdy. The portions knocked into the ground will need treating with a preservative like Cuprinol if they're not to rot in a short period.

Cane fruits like raspberries, and restricted forms of top fruit such as cordons, espaliers and fans, will need solid upright supports in angle-iron or wood and/or horizontal wires, which should be plastic-covered or galvanised for long life.

If you're planting fan-trained fruit, you'll need substantial rawlplugs for inserting into brickwork or masonry; alternatively, provide suitable brass or galvanised screws for fixing into wooden fences.

If wires are to be strung between angle-iron or wooden posts, purchase the appropriate amount of galvanised ring bolts for fixing.

Supports for rows of cane fruits and individual fan-trained trees need to go into position before planting, but free-standing top trees can be staked as you plant.

In most areas, a single substantial stake will suffice for most top fruit, but where there is a fierce prevailing wind, a second stake should be inserted at an angle to the upright, on the leeward side of the tree.

Also make sure you have sufficient tree ties. Hessian bands and strong string will suffice, but adjustable plastic ties are best if you can afford them.

The tie should be nailed to the support (not the tree) in exposed windy areas to avoid bark chafing.

1 Check all plants immediately they arrive and soak thoroughly before you plant them.

2 Cut off any broken or dead roots with a sharp knife or secateurs to prevent them rotting once established.

3 Sprinkle some general fertiliser over the base of the planting hole and gently fork in.

4 Plastic containers should be cut away from the root-ball. Tin containers are normally pre-cut at the garden centre.

5 Once the root-ball is at the right level, gradually fill in with good topsoil or compost, firming as you go.

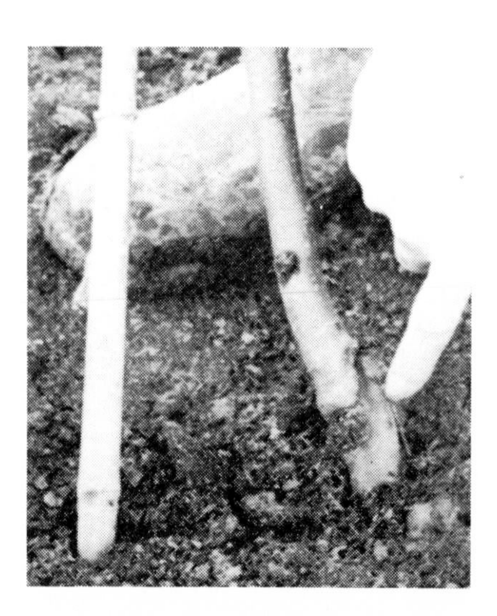

6 Top fruit, like apples, that has been grafted should be planted so that the 'union' is above the soil level.

Planting cordons

1 Cordon apples and pears must be planted at an angle of 45 degrees. A cane to which they are tied is put in at the same time.

2 A strong cross-wire is needed to which the cane is tied.

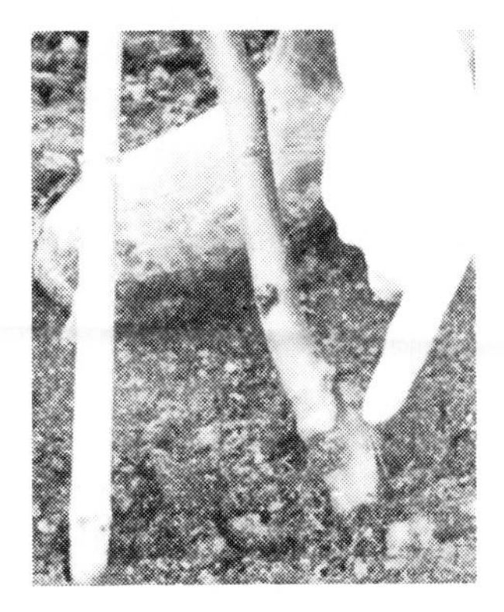

3 The union must be clear of the surrounding soil when planting is finished.

4 The finished job. Cordons should be 2–3ft (60–90cm) apart.

Planting currants

1 Soak bush-fruit roots thoroughly before planting, then check over for any damaged ones. These should be carefully cut off with a sharp knife or secateurs.

2 Make sure the planting hole is wide enough to take roots spread out from the centre. On poor shallow soils overlying chalk, plant blackcurrants at an angle of 45 degrees.

3 Try to plant blackcurrants so that three or four buds are buried to form a good underground framework. Prune back to leave one bud showing. Space 5ft (1.5m) apart, or 30in (75cm) apart for cordons.

Staking trees

From October on we can expect strong winds, so it is wise to check stakes and ties on all fruit trees, paying particular attention to newly-planted ones that have not had time to establish a good root system for firm anchorage.

1 Where fruit-tree ties have deteriorated and are liable to snap in windy weather, they will need replacing with something more substantial. Remove the old tie and check the firmness of the supporting stake.

2 In exposed positions, newly-planted trees are prone to severe root disturbance because of wind rock; therefore angle the stake to face into the prevailing wind. Fasten a strong plastic tie to the tree and support it so that it is held firmly, but not tightly.

3 Finally, nail the tie to the stake to prevent it working loose. When you are checking ties, look at the condition of the stakes and replace any that are rotting and liable to snap off.

Blackcurrants from cuttings

A hedge of blackcurrants will make an attractive and productive border to the fruit or vegetable patch. New plants are easily raised from cuttings taken at pruning time.

1 Newly planted bushes should be cut right back to two or three buds from the ground, as should fruited branches of established bushes.

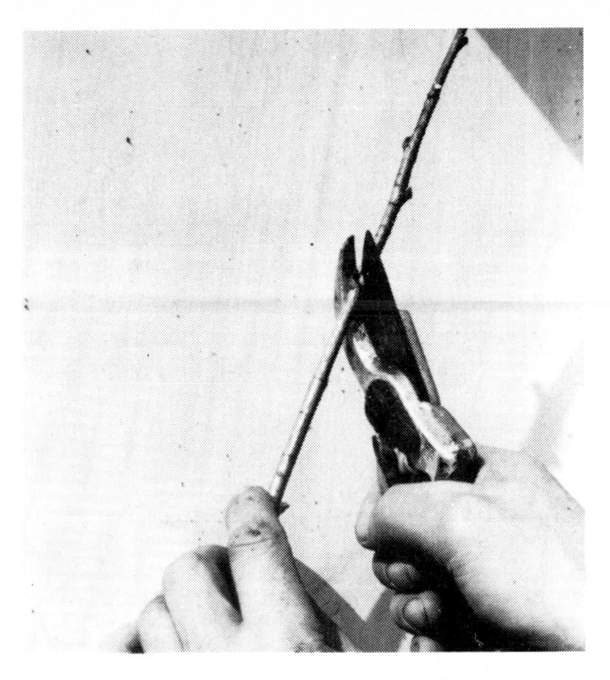

2 Use these stems as cuttings. If possible, choose wood from the current season's growth, but if this is scarce, use older wood. Trim to 10in (25cm) long, cutting at a leaf joint, top and bottom.

3 Make a slit trench about 6in (15cm) deep, along the line of the required hedge. Alternatively, set the cuttings in a corner of the garden to provide single plants.

4 Push the cuttings into the trench, leaving about 4in (10cm) of the shoot out of the ground. Cuttings should be placed about 6in (15cm) apart.

5 Refill the trench and firm the soil round the cuttings with your heel. Set a few extra cuttings at the end of the row to replace failures.

Planting strawberries

Strawberry runners you have rooted yourself or bought in can be planted in August or September, or any time into autumn, while soil conditions are favourable. Give them as much organic material as possible and keep them growing to build up into strong plants for fruiting next year.

1 Where you have rooted runners from healthy stock plants, cut the stem that has been the lifeline for the young strawberry plant.

2 Remove all weeds from the planting site and apply a generous layer of organic material like rotted manure, compost or proprietary products like Forest Bark or Super Manure.

3 After digging in the organic material, dress the ground with fertiliser (not required if Super Manure is used) and rake level. Tread down light soils to settle ground.

4 Use a line to space out runners 15–18in (38–45cm) apart in the rows. Space rows out not less than 30in (75cm) apart.

5 Plant runners so that the crown is not buried and firm in by hand. The compost surface should be level with the ground.

6 Well water in the runners after planting and keep the site moist to enable the plants to get established rapidly. Regularly hoe down the rows to aerate soil and prevent weed growth.

Colour
Lettuce 'Great Lakes' – as it is particularly loathe to bolt, this is an ideal variety to grow in those long, hot, dry summers . . . if we ever get another one! (Picture: Ian and Stuart Unwin)

Strawberries in grow-bags

There is no reason why you should not enjoy strawberries, whether you have a garden or not. This fruit will give excellent crops in a wide range of containers, but remember to de-blossom them in the first spring after planting. Suitable containers for strawberries include growing bags, barrels, tower pots or 'verti-strawb' polythene 'sausages'.

1 Once your strawberry runners arrive, give them a good soak before planting them in either the open ground or containers filled with a rich compost.

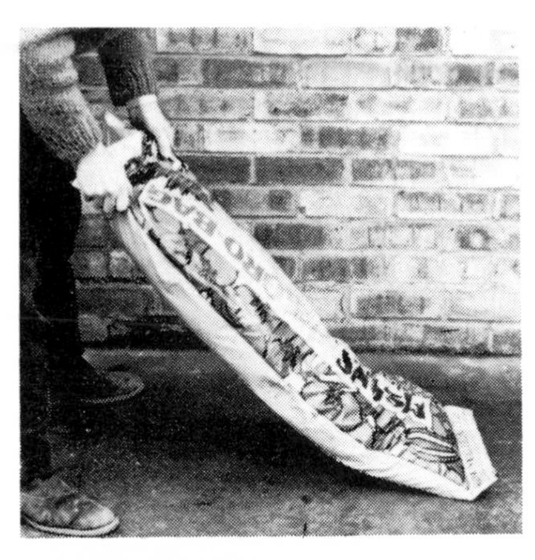

2 Growing bags are suitable for strawberries if you don't have any room in the garden. Make sure that the compost is distributed evenly by shaking the bag.

3 Make from eight to ten cross-incisions in the sides where the plants are to go, on the 'shoulder' of the bag.

4 Use your hands to form a hole in the compost and gently ease the runners into the planting positions. Firm down so that the crown is not buried.

5 Make a slit along the top of the bag to allow watering, but unless you intend to use this area for growing a few lettuces, etc, do not fold the flaps back.

Colour
Leek 'Catalina' – the flavour's mild, so this variety should be acceptable no matter how finicky your family's tastes are. Remains in good condition in the ground until required for use (Picture: Dobies Seeds)

Raising strawberries from runners

There's no reason why you should not raise your own young strawberry plants from runners, provided the parent stock has large and healthy foliage. If your plants are old or look pale and stunted, pull them up and start with fresh stock this autumn or next spring.

1 Strawberry runners will provide new plants for planting out next spring. If the plants are in containers, prepare small pots of well-drained compost.

2 Pin down the tips of runners using a hairpin or piece of wire. Plants in the open ground can be increased in similar fashion or pegged directly into the soil.

3 As the parent plant will be putting on new growth and supporting runner development, feed weekly using a complete balanced fertiliser and keep the compost well watered.

4 Once the plants have finished fruiting, remove old leaves and excess runners (all of them if new plants are not required). Burn all rubbish, including straw round outside plants.

5 Keep new foliage clear of pests, especially sucking insects like aphids which can carry virus diseases. Some insecticides must not be used on strawberries, so check the labels carefully

Pruning apples

Now that new growth is well developed on apples, prune back lateral shoots to encourage flowering next year; on large trees, prune back to about 5in (12–13cm). Continue pest and disease control, de-suckering and watering when necessary.

1 Apples, when trained in a restricted form like cordons, will need some summer pruning. Reduce lateral shoots back to the third leaf (ignore the cluster of leaves at the base).

2 Don't prune the leading shoots on restricted forms of apple. This is particularly important for young trees, as they give the extension growth for height.

3 Although the 'June drop' will thin out fruitlets naturally, you may still need to reduce numbers on prolific bearers. For good fruiting, allow 4–6in (10–15cm) between them.

4 Remove suckers that appear at the base of trees as close to the rootstock as possible. If left, they will rob the tree of food and develop into a thicket of unwanted growth.

5 It's important that fruit trees do not suffer from a lack of water, so to improve fruit yields, soak the roots thoroughly in dry periods. Pay special attention to newly planted trees.

6 Give preventative sprays of fenitrothion (Fentro) or malathion to discourage codling moth grubs in fruitlets: BHC/malathion/dimethoate (Super Kil) will control codling moth and red spider.

Root pruning

Established top fruit may sometimes show great vigour but fail to give a satisfactory crop. This can sometimes be rectified by summer pruning, but if this fails you may have to resort to pruning the roots. On old trees, it pays to root prune in two stages, working on one side of the tree in the first year, and the other side in the following winter.

1 Use a line to mark out the position of the trench round the tree. Depending on the size of the tree, the trench should be between 2 and 4ft (60cm and 1.2m) from the trunk.

2 `Take out the trench round half of the tree, exposing the root system. Sever the smaller roots at the outer trench wall but take care not to damage the lengths of root.

3 Remove the larger roots with a saw. If there are many small roots, tie these back towards the tree to give a free working area in the trench.

4 When all the large roots have been removed, replace some of the soil and tread down firmly. Small roots that have been tied back out of the way can now be replaced in the trench.

5 Gradually refill the trench with soil, well firming in as you go to prevent air spaces round the roots. If the tree is in a grassed area, relay any turves that were lifted.

Gooseberries from cuttings

Gooseberry cuttings should be taken in October, even if the leaves are still on the plants. Select healthy young shoots from the current season's growth. They should be about 8in (20cm) long.

1 To avoid suckering, the buds should be removed from all but the top 2in (5cm). Use the point of a sharp knife.

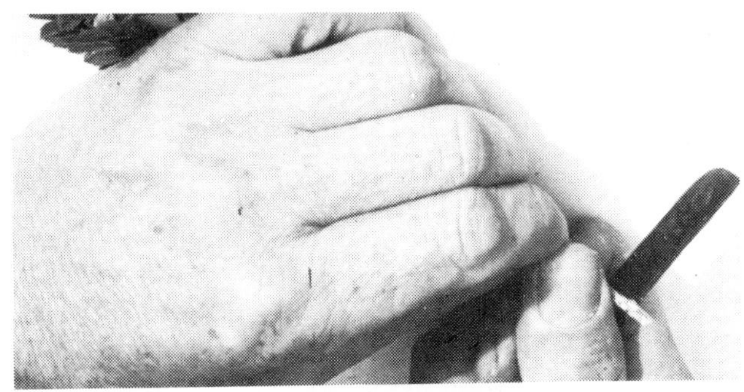

2 Trim the base of the cutting just below a leaf joint. There should be no need to use rooting powder.

3 Select a sheltered spot and make a slit by working a spade backwards and forwards in the soil.

4 A little sharp sand in the bottom of the hole will help rooting. Don't use builder's sand.

5 Set the cuttings about 6in (15cm) apart and about 4in (10cm) deep, with the base resting on the sand.

6 Refill the slit trench and firm the cuttings in well with your boot.

Herbs

Herbs are often neglected by the vegetable gardener, yet many of us find them just as important as the more common vegetable-garden plants. New potatoes need to be cooked with sprigs of fresh mint; parsley sauce adds delicious flavour to almost every fish dish.

So even if you haven't room for a separate and properly laid-out herb garden, it's well worth finding space for a few plants in a corner of the veg patch. Most of them are hardy, surviving with ease the most unkind of weather, and they are seldom afflicted by pests and diseases.

Apart from mint, culinary herbs flourish happily together, so a whole mass of them can be grown in a comparatively small space. The problem with mint is its rampant root system, which can soon force out any plants near it; so grow mint well away from everything else or, better still, plant it in large pots to contain the spread of its roots.

In the main, herbs are grown in exactly the same way as vegetables. But there are two important points to remember.

First, more care has to be taken with watering than with vegetables, over-watering being just as bad as no water.

Second, until they are well established, cut them only gently. A major point in their favour is that many are perennial, so once an area of herbs is established it will need little care and maintenance beyond re-sowing a few annuals such as parsley and dill.

Culinary herbs

Thousands of herbs are known to man and they fall into three main groups - medicinal, cosmetic and culinary. It is the latter group, of course, that has a place in the vegetable garden. Listed below are those that have proved most popular with gardeners over the centuries and that will be of greatest use to housewives.

Angelica
Grows 3–5ft (1–1.5m) tall and thrives in partial shade. A handsome plant, it is very attractive to bees. Its young stems can be crystallized for use as a trifle or cake decoration, and the leaves added to stewed fruit to reduce tartness.

Sow seeds outdoors in August or early September, transplanting to the cropping position as soon as the plants can be handled. Space them 18in (45cm) apart.

Pick the young stems in April or May, and the leaves in May and June.

Basil
This has a nutmeg flavour and is chiefly used with tomato dishes such as pizzas, salads and aspic. Some stems should be dried for winter use, though it tastes better used fresh.

Sow the seeds in warmth in March or April, pricking-out into boxes. Harden them off in a cold frame or sheltered spot in the garden before planting out 8in (20cm) apart in early June. Basil prefers a warm growing position and favours a light but rich soil. It is wise to pinch out the tops to encourage leafiness.

Cut off the stems when flowers appear, and either use the stems fresh or tie them in bunches and dry them in a dark cupboard.

Caraway (*biennial*)
Grows 1–2ft (30–60cm) tall and produces tiny spicy seeds used as flavouring in cakes, bread and buns. The seeds can also be used in pickles and coleslaws.

Sow the seeds direct into the ground in March in rows 1ft (30cm) apart. When the plants have grown 2–3in (5–7cm) high, thin them to leave 10in (25cm) between each plant.

In the following year, pick the flower clusters when they are fully developed, lay them to dry on paper and shake out the seeds.

Dill (*annual*)
Although a native of the Mediterranean region, dill is easily grown in Britain. Grows 1½–2ft (45–60cm) high. The leaves are used for flavouring soups, and to flavour potatoes and peas in the same way as mint. The seeds may be used in seed cakes and for making pickles.

In March, sow the seeds direct into the ground ¾in (2cm) deep and when the plants are big enough to handle, thin them to 9in (23cm) apart.

Harvest the flower heads as they ripen, hanging them up to dry before shaking out the seeds, which should be kept in an airtight jar. Use young leaves for flavouring, pulling them off the plant as and when they are needed.

Fennel (*perennial*)
Produces fern-like leaves and grows 4–6ft (1.2–1.8m) high. The leaves can be cooked with fish (for example, mackerel has a far better flavour when boiled with fennel), or chopped up and mixed into a white sauce for boiled fish. The dried seeds can be used to flavour both fish and soups.

Sow in April or May direct into the ground, thinning the seedlings to 1ft (30cm) apart and grow them in clumps of several plants. To obtain a regular supply of young and tender new leaves, cut the stems down three or four times during the growing season to encourage new growth. When the clumps reach a good size, split them with a spade and replant the offsets.

Pull off the young leaves as and when they are required, and harvest the seeds in the same way as dill.

Garlic (*annual*)
You either love it or hate it - but there's no doubt it adds a distinctive flavour to all dishes it is used in. And one of the best ways to use it is to turn the cloves into garlic vinegar.

Plant the cloves (segments stripped from garlic bulbs) in a light, fertilised soil, 9in (23cm) apart and buried so that only the tip is showing.

Lift the crop in August or September when the foliage turns yellow and withers. Lay them out to dry (outdoors if the weather is good) and then store the bulbs in a dry, cool but frost-proof place.

Horseradish (*perennial*)
Homemade horseradish sauce is more pungent and less peppery than the sauce you buy in shops. To make it, simply grate the roots into a little whipped cream. The one growing problem with horseradish is that it can spread like wildfire; a way of getting over this problem is to grow it in raised beds.

In March, dig a trench 2–2½ft (60–75cm) deep and dig in fresh manure or compost and fine soil into the bottom. Plant pieces of root 15in (38cm) deep and 1ft (30cm) apart. Remove all sideshoots as the plants grow, leaving only the terminal growth. The roots need to be 10–12in (25–30cm) long when pulled for use, and this will usually take 2 or 3 years.

Dig up the roots as required, or harvest the whole crop and store the roots in sand in a dry, frost-proof shed.

Lovage (*perennial*)
An attractive plant that grows to around 4ft (1.2m). Its flavour is similar to that of celery and the leaves can be added to soups, stews and salads.

Sow the seeds direct into the ground in March, choosing a shady, moist position. Thin out the plants as soon as they are big enough to handle to 3ft (90cm) apart.

Pull off young, tender leaves as required.

Marjoram (*annual*)
There are several marjorams and they are used to flavour pizzas, salads, omelettes and vinegar. Grows 1–2ft (30–60cm) high.

Prepare a sowing bed by working a light compost into the soil and sow the seeds ½in (1–2cm) deep; thin the plants to 1ft (30cm) apart. Germination can be poor, so it may be necessary to make repeat sowings in late spring and early summer.

Pull the young, tender leaves as required until just before the plant comes into full flower in July. Hang up the leaves to dry, then rub the leaves into small pieces and store them in air-tight jars.

Mint (*perennial*)
Used to make mint sauce (simply chop up a handful of leaves, mix in a teaspoon of sugar and then add just enough vinegar to make liquid), and used fresh to flavour new potatoes and peas. Mint freezes well, but tends to lose its colour.

To restrict its rampant roots, grow it in large pots of soil. Plant roots 2in (5cm) deep in March and keep the plants well-watered.

Pull off the leaves or sprigs as and when required.

Parsley (*biennial*)
Rich in vitamins, parsley can be used for making a sauce, fresh in salads and even deep-fried to be served as a cooked vegetable. It is probably the most popular of flavouring herbs.

Sow in shallow drills in March in soil fortified with manure or compost. The rows should be 1ft

(30cm) apart and when the plants are big enough to handle, thin them out to 3in (7cm) apart. Make further sowings in May and July, and cover a row or two with cloches in October to make sure of fresh supplies during severe winters.

Do not strip individual plants of all their leaves – just cut off sprigs here and there as and when required. Parsley for drying should be gathered in July or August and dried by spreading them out on a fire-proof tray above a cooker. The dried parsley should then be rubbed between the fingers and bottled at once.

Sage (*perennial*)
The strong, fragrant leaves of this evergreen bush herb are dried and used to make stuffing – but be careful with the amount you use as the flavour of sage can override that of any other herbs in the mixture.

It's best to grow from plants bought from a nursery, but some types of sage can also be grown from seed. Sow in March or April, thinning the seedlings to 2in (5cm) apart before moving the plants to their final growing positions when they are growing well. The plants like an open, sunny position and a layer of compost should be forked into the top 1in (2–3cm) of soil.

Gather the leaves as required and dry them by laying them on a fire-proof tray above a cooker. Then rub the dried leaves from the stalks and store in a dry place.

Savory (*perennial*)
Another powerfully flavoured herb that can be used for stuffings and in salad dressings. It is a low-grower and its leaves can be picked fresh all the year.

Savory favours a sunny, well-drained soil that must not be too rich in humus as this will promote lush growth which will not stand the winter. It can be grown from either seeds or plants: seeds should be sown in April and thinned out to 1ft (30cm) apart when they are large enough to handle, and plants should be put in during April or May 1ft (30cm) apart.

Take off the foliage as and when required, drying it by hanging it indoors or outdoors in the sun. Rub the dried herb between the hands and store in a dry place.

Tarragon (*perennial*)
Mainly associated with chicken dishes, it can be used during cooking to add flavour or in sauces and stuffings. It is a low, bushy shrub with fine-cut grey foliage.

Choose a dry, light area and sow the seeds in April in drills 1in (2–3cm) deep. As the plants develop, thin them out to 1ft (30cm) apart and protect the plants during winter by mulching with compost, manure or peat.

Pick the leaves as required, dry and crumble them, and then store them in a dry place.

Thyme (*perennial*)
A long-term evergreen herb, thyme – like sage – should be used sparingly as its aroma is strong. Its main use is as a stuffing ingredient, but it can also be used with parsley and bay leaves to make a traditional bouquet garni.

Thyme likes a light soil and a sunny position. Sow the seeds fairly thinly ½in (1–2cm) deep in April, thinning the plants out to 1ft (30cm) apart. Spare seedlings can be transplanted. An easy way of propagating from established bushes is to dig up a plant, tear off the rooted offsets and replant them 1ft (30cm) apart.

Fresh thyme can be picked from spring to November. Take a sprig here and there from each plant, and wash before use. For storing, hang sprigs out to dry, rub the foliage between the hands, and store in containers in a dry place.

Growing chives and garlic

Chives and garlic are two of our most popular herbs. They are both planted in April, and chives can also be raised from seed.

1 Container-grown herbs such as chives should be planted in well-dug soil.

2 Overcrowded clumps of chives can also be lifted and divided into small groups of about 6 bulbs each. They like a sunny position. Pick out the blooms as they appear.

3 When growing garlic, break up the bulbs into individual cloves ready for planting in well-drained soil in full sun.

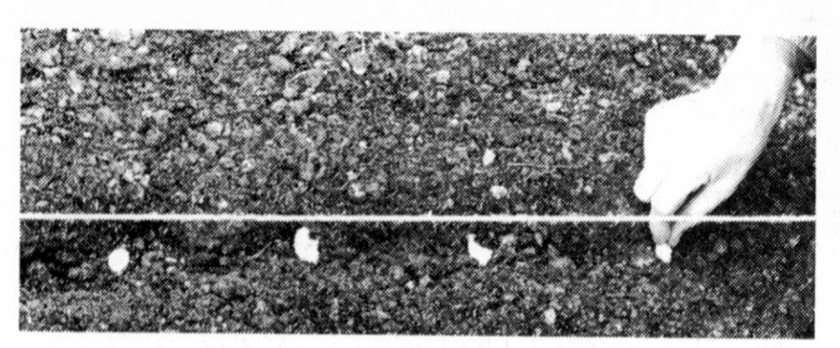

4 Take out a drill 2in (5cm) deep and push the cloves into these at 6in (15cm) intervals. If more than one row is needed, space these 1ft (30cm) apart.

Chives . . . they're excellent in salads as an alternative to spring onions, which have a far stronger flavour.

You either love it or hate it – but there's no doubt that garlic adds a distinctive flavour to all dishes it is used in.

Pests and Diseases

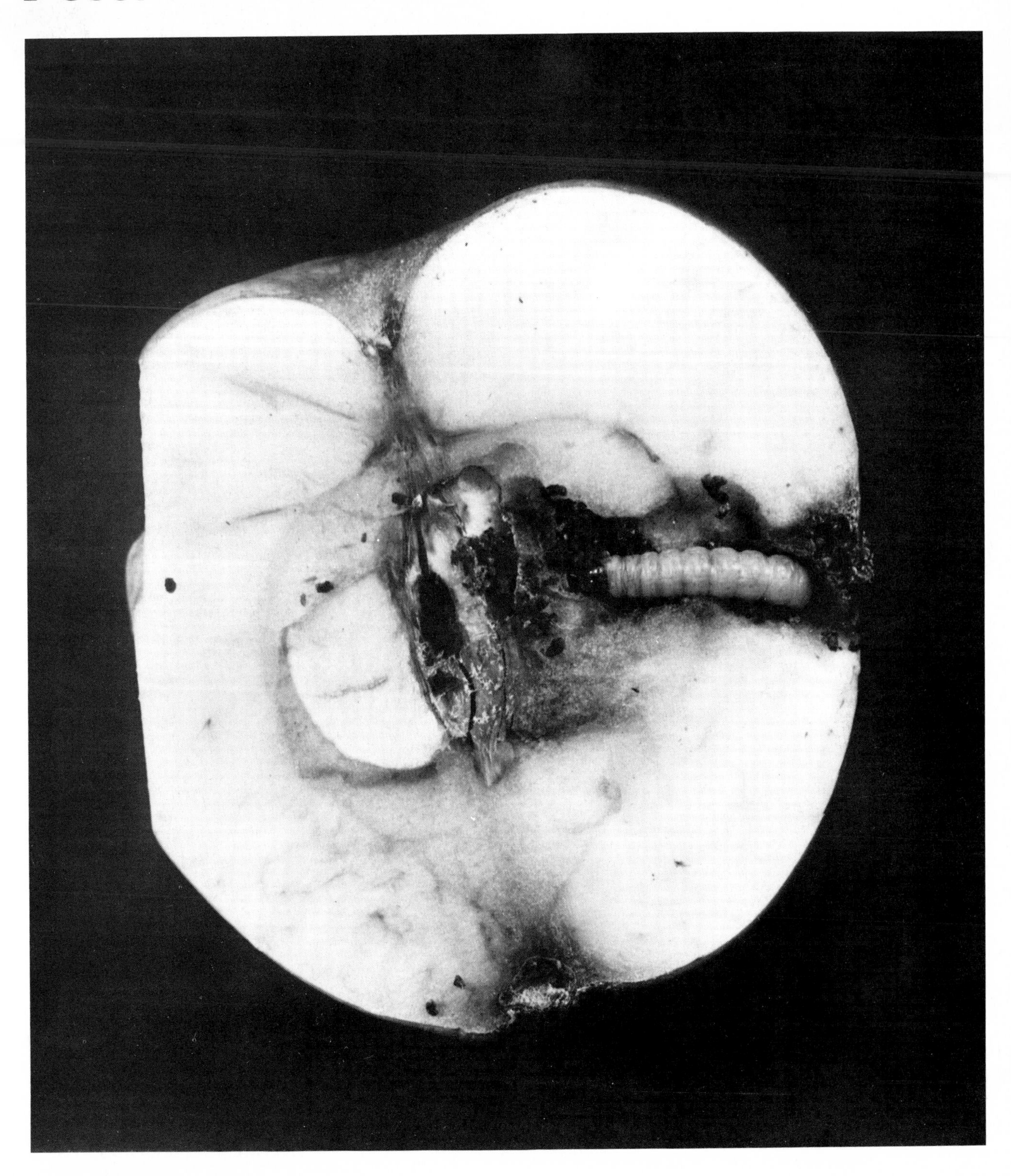

Aphids

Applying derris dust to broad beans in May to keep aphids at bay.

Apple sawfly

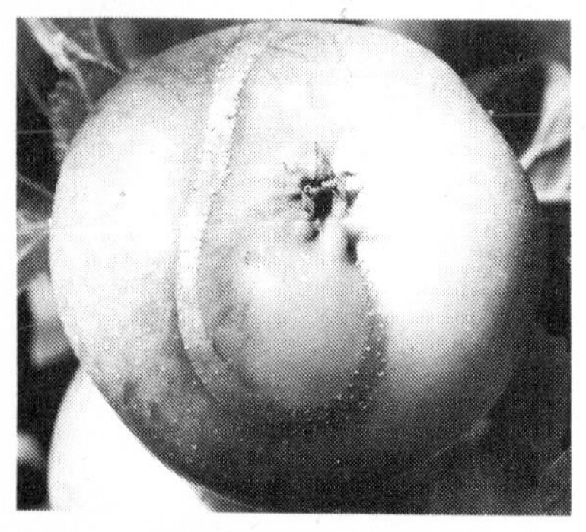

Grubs attack in June; they should not be confused with the codling moth whose grubs attack in July and August.

Young grubs leave a sticky mess on the outside of fruitlet where they enter, then burrow just under the skin leaving a ribbon-like scar. The maggot leaves the fruit through another hole in July. The appearance of the fruit is spoiled at the very least. Attacked apples may drop off when quite young.

Spray trees with BHC or systemic insecticide when most of the petals have fallen. Timing is important.

Apple scab

A common and serious disease of all apples.

Small black spots appear on young fruits, spreading into blackened areas that often crack. Brown spots also occur on leaves. The general disfiguration of the fruit sometimes spreads to young shoots of trees.

Lime sulphur or systemic fungicide sprays must be applied at regular intervals, starting at green blossom-bud stage, again at pink-bud stage, at petal fall and often again three weeks later.

Black spot

A common fungus disease of roses.

The fungus starts in the spring as black specks on leaves which increase in size and become most noticeable in mid and late summer. Leaves drop prematurely in bad attacks, and bushes are severely weakened.

Gather up and burn all affected leaves. Spray with tar-oil wash in winter to kill spores. Spray at fourteen-day intervals through spring and summer with systemic fungicide or collodial copper.

Cabbage root fly

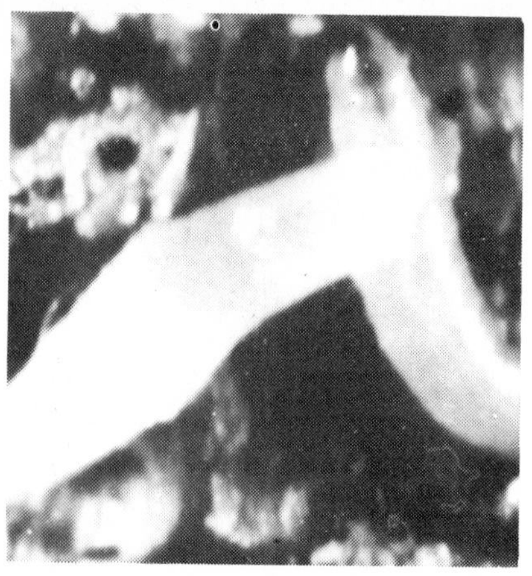

All brassicas are liable to attack, particularly in April and May, but are vulnerable all summer. Eggs are laid just below soil surface round plants.

Maggots eat and damage the main roots. Plants wilt and turn blue. Badly attacked plants shrivel and die, particularly in hot dry weather.

Dust seed-beds with calomel dust, which should be applied round newly set out plants. Use soil insecticides in the same way.

Canker parsnip

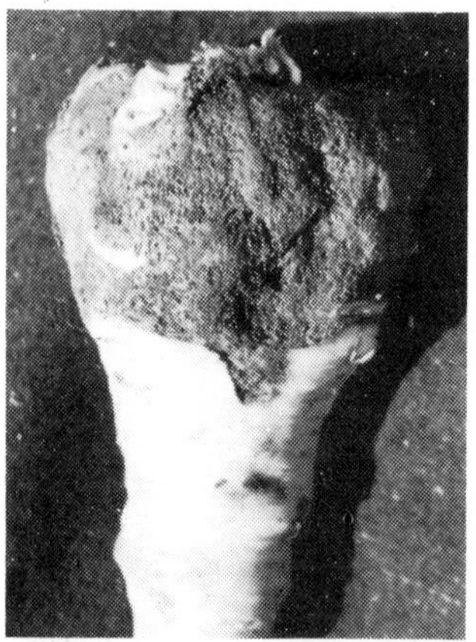

Brown patches which start around soil level and spread.

The canker enters the root through cracks or damage caused by pests. Bad attacks can make parsnips unusable.

Grow resistant varieties. Use soil insecticides to deter attacks of carrot fly, which can start the disease.

Carrot fly

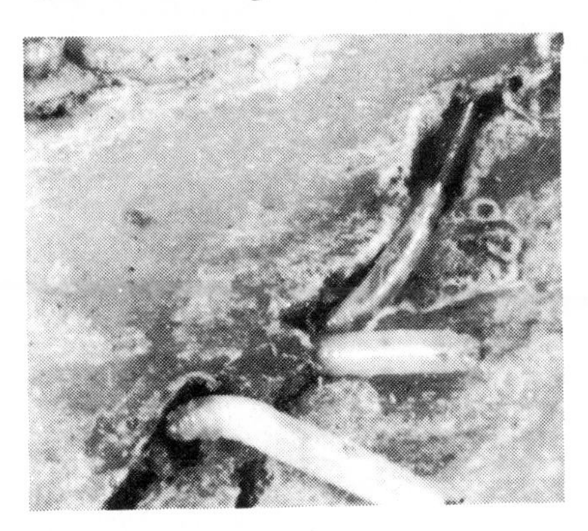

Fly which lays eggs in May around carrots, just under the surface of the soil.

Damage is caused by small maggots, which bore into roots. Seedlings will wilt and die. Reddening leaves are a sign of attack. Parsnips, parsley and celery are also liable to attack.

Soil insecticides should be applied before sowing and along the sides of the rows in April and May.

Club root

A fungus that attacks all brassicas and can live for several years in the ground.

Roots become swollen and distorted, often splitting and rotting to give off offensive smell. Plants are stunted and dwarfed yet generally manage to keep alive.

Apply dressings of lime to sweeten sour soils. Pay attention to crop rotations. Dress seed-beds with calomel dust and sprinkle it in holes where plants are going.

Codling moth

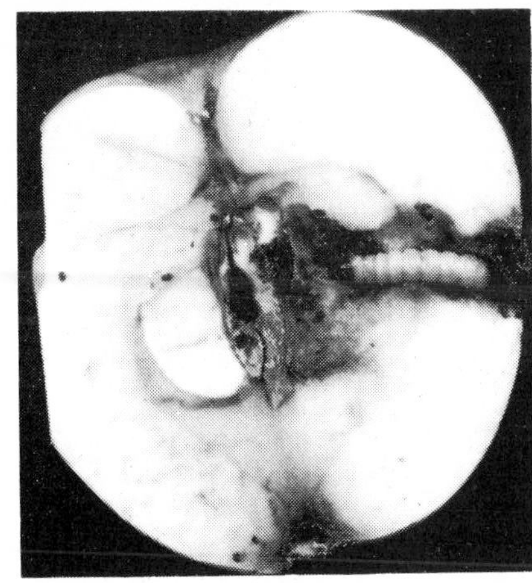

The 'grub' that is found in the centre of mature apples, as opposed to the sawfly maggot that drops out of the fruit in the summer.

The grub generally enters the fruit in or near the eye. Fruit often drops just before ripening and will not keep.

Sacking or corrugated cardboard tied in bands round the trunks in July will trap the hibernating caterpillars. Remove and burn during winter. Spray fruits with Fentro in July.

Flea beetle

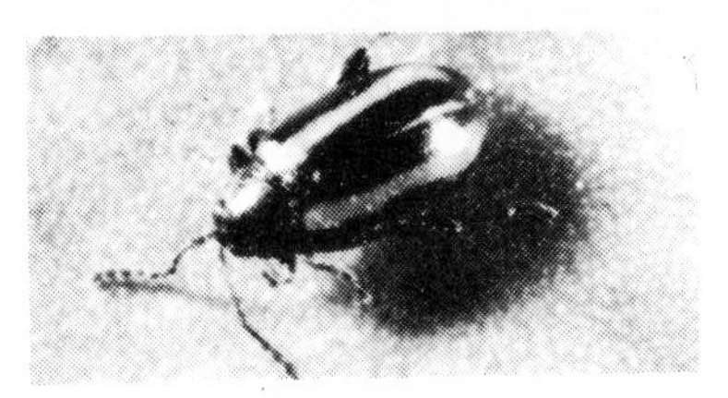

Serious pest of all brassica family doing most damage on young plants.

Small flea-like creatures that attack seed-beds, making holes in young leaves during warm sunny spells in

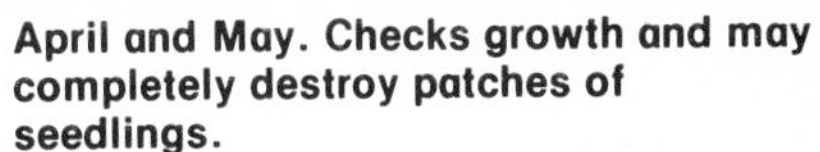

April and May. Checks growth and may completely destroy patches of seedlings.

Dust rows of seedlings as they appear with derris and repeat until plants are 2–3in (5–8cm) high.

Flea beetles can be a real menace on turnips. Spray to deter them.

Green capsid bug

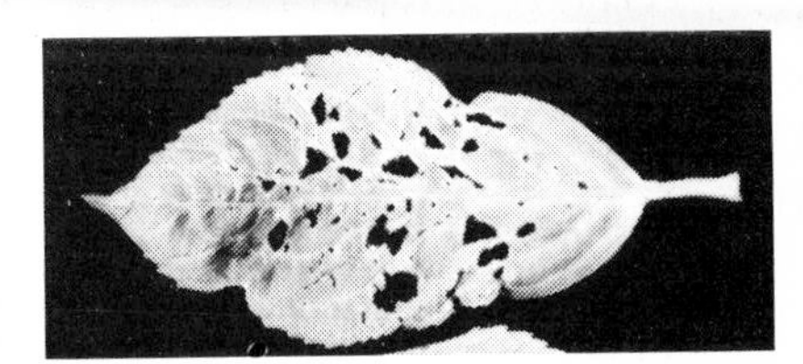

Attacks many plants but particularly fruit trees and bushes, chrysanthemums, dahlias, roses and beans.

Rather like big greenfly but does not congregate in great numbers. First attacks show as spots on the leaves, which turn into holes as the leaves grow. Growing plants are deformed and damaged. Young leaves turn brown and stop growing.

Apply derris or malathion dust to the tips of shoots during May and June.

Greenfly

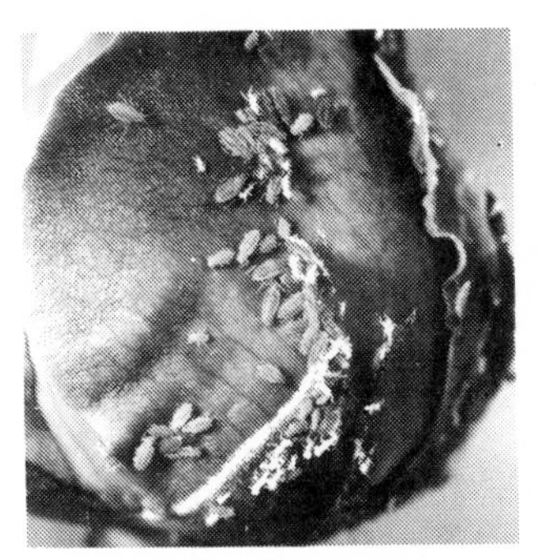

Most common plant pest, attacking almost all plants, but is one of the most easily controlled.

Green winged and wingless insects congregate in great numbers in flowers or near growing-tips of plants. Plants and shoots are weakened and distorted and virus disease is spread from affected to clean plants.

Spray with various insecticides at intervals through spring and summer. Use systemic insecticides and fumigate frames and greenhouses.

Leaf miner

Attacks weeds, which act as hosts, as well as cultivated plants.

Fly punctures leaf to lay eggs, which become tunnelling maggots. White spots are first signs, followed by distinctive trails. Plants are weakened and in bad attacks leaves are lost.

Hand-pick maggots in slight attacks. Spray with malathion or nicotine.

Leather jackets

Larvae of the daddy-long-legs, which feed on all kinds of roots.

Tough-skinned, legless and about an inch long. Because eggs are laid among grass, they are often a bad pest where lawns and fields are newly dug. Growth of all plants is affected as roots are eaten. Dead patches appear on lawns.

Apply sevin or BHC dust mixed with sand from October to April.

Mealy bug

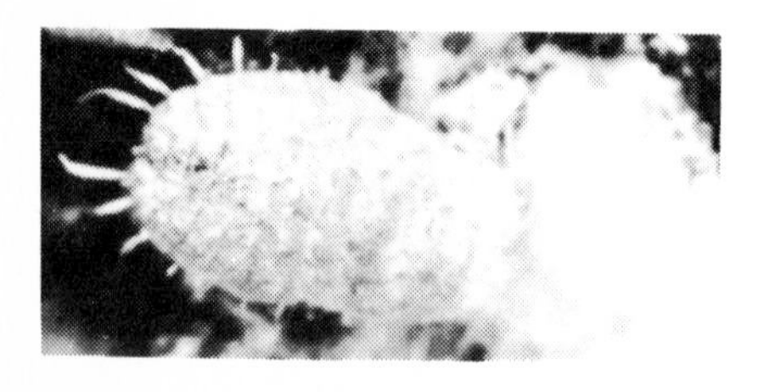

Infests trees, shrubs, greenhouse plants, vines and cacti.

Grey insects appear in cracks and joints of plants, which are often covered with a white mealy substance. There is a loss of vigour, yellowing and loss of leaves in severe attacks.

Forcible spray with malathion or malathion dust.

Mildew

Affects many plants but most commonly recognised on roses.

Starts as grey spots on young leaves but quickly spreads over all the new growth. Growth is retarded and flowering checked.

Spray at intervals from April onwards with a rose mildew specific.

Raspberry beetle

Attacks the fruit of raspberries, blackberries and loganberries.

Generally only recognised by the small grubs that are found in the fruit when it is picked. Damages the fruit.

Spray or dust fruit trusses with derris; middle and end of June for raspberries and loganberries, early and mid July for blackberries.

Red Spider

Whatever you do, keep red spiders away from your crops. They are making a real mess of this cucumber plant. They thrive in over-dry conditions.

Scale insects

There are many types but damage is similar in all cases. They attack all shrubs and trees and various greenhouse plants.

Non-active, remaining firmly attached in one place on twigs, branches, under leaves; like small shells. Plants lose vigour. Some species produce a honeydew on which black sooty mould develops.

In winter, dormant, deciduous trees and shrubs can be sprayed with tar-oil wash, otherwise use systemic insecticide.

Slugs

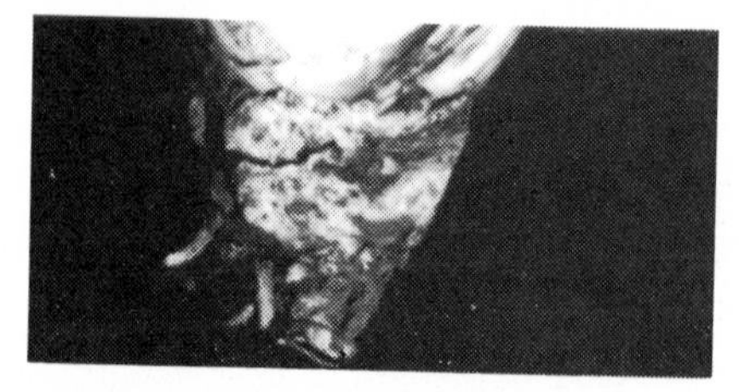

Will damage all kinds of plants by feeding on leaves, stems and roots. Particularly bad in poorly drained soils.

Mainly two types: keeled slugs, which feed on underground parts, and field slugs, which eat leaves and stems. They can completely destroy the garden.

Use slug pellets or liquid wherever attacks may occur.

Pellets such as these will keep slugs at bay – in both the ornamental and vegetable garden.

Tomato leaf mould

Most common on indoor tomatoes, appearing generally in June.

Attacks older leaves first, appearing as pale patches on upper surfaces and later as purple or brown patches on lower leaves. Can shrivel leaves completely. Flowers are sometimes affected, but the main trouble is a general weakening effect.

Grow resistant strains. Provide adequate ventilation. Pick off and burn affected leaves. Spray with systemic fungicide.

Vine weevil

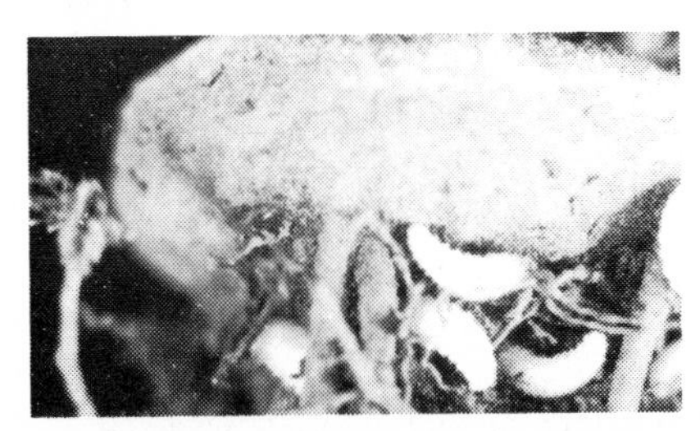

Larvae and adults attack many kinds of plants, including cyclamen, cinerarias, begonias, ferns in pots and rhododendrons, alpines, strawberries and raspberries.

Larvae are fat legless grubs, creamy white with a large head. Adults, which feed at night, are black covered with short hairs and about half an inch long. Larvae attack roots and underground stems. Adults feed on leaves at night. Root attacks cause wilting, leaf attacks weaken and disfigure.

Dust or spray with insecticides. Repot plants attacked into fresh compost, or use soil insecticides.

White fly

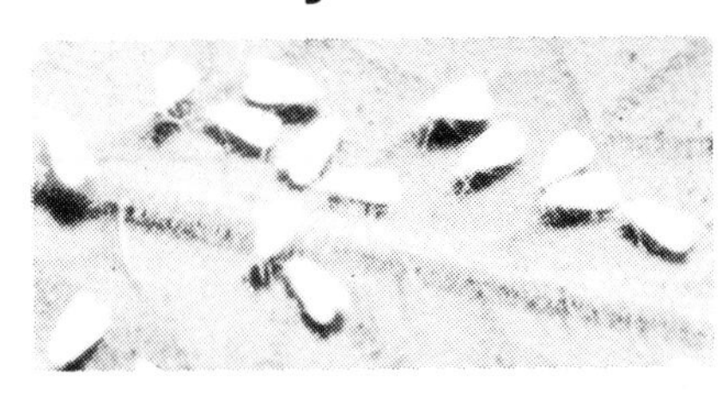

Pest of greenhouse plants and brassicas in the open garden.

Small white moth-like insects, which congregate on undersides of leaves and fly up in smothers when disturbed. They cause a general weakening of plants, also leaving sticky substance on which moulds grow.

Repeat sprays of white-fly insecticide at intervals of 7–10 days to catch hatching eggs.

Wood lice

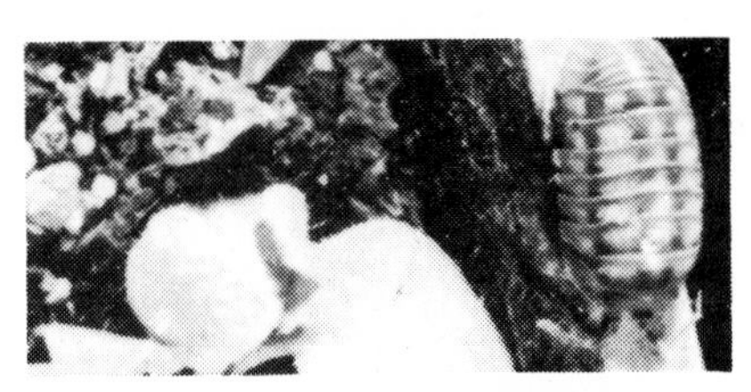

Generally found where rubbish collects, particularly in greenhouses.

Oval, half-inch-long, dark-grey insects with legs and feelers; roll up into a ball when touched. They will gnaw at all parts of plants, eating holes in leaves.

Avoid accumulating rubbish, and dust-frequented places with derris or BHC dust.

Woolly aphis

A pest mainly of apple trees but will also affect ornamental trees and shrubs; also known as American blight.

Insects appear on shoots and branches are covered with a white wool-like substance. Shoots become swollen and distorted and the plant's general vigour is decreased.

Wash dormant trees with tar-oil and forcibly apply insecticides during growing season. Small patches can be painted with a brush.

Freezing

Young and tender

When freezing vegetables, always choose young and tender produce – and freeze as soon as possible after harvesting. Produce that is only second-rate when fresh will be third-rate after freezing.

If you are growing vegetables specially for the freezer, go for varieties that are recommended for freezing. Many mail-order companies list in their catalogues varieties that freeze particularly well.

Blanching

In the charts on pages 157–61 blanching times are given as part of the freezing instructions for many fruits and vegetables.

Blanching is scalding the produce in boiling water for a short time to prevent deterioration in the colour, flavour and texture of the fruit and vegetables.

Recommended blanching times should be adhered to since over-blanching and under-blanching are equally harmful.

The picture sequence on page 162 gives the method to be adopted for blanching cauliflowers, and most vegetables must be blanched if they are to retain their quality for any length of time in the freezer. This is because freezing alone is not sufficient to inactivate the enzymes contained in the vegetables.

In addition, blanching has the advantage of reducing the natural turgidity of the vegetables, particularly of the leafy varieties, thus making them easy to pack into containers or bags.

The water in the blanching container must be boiling rapidly, the quantity required being 6–8 pints (3½–4½ litres) of water to blanch 1lb (454gm) vegetables. The same water can be used for successive batches.

If the vegetables impart a strong flavour to the blanching water, as cauliflower and spinach do, it may be necessary to change the water more frequently. A kettle of boiling water should be kept on hand for topping-up.

The blanching basket containing the vegetables should be plunged into the boiling water, and it may be necessary to use an enamel lid to keep the vegetables submerged.

The blanching time is measured from the moment that the water in the container returns to full boil. This must not take more than 1 minute. Check this carefully when adding the first batch of vegetables, and if the recovery time is slower than 1 minute reduce the weight of subsequent batches accordingly.

When blanching is finished, drain the basket, then cool and chill the vegetables as quickly as possible in a bowl of cold water to which ice has been added. Thorough chilling is essential if a high quality of blanching is to be achieved.

When the vegetables feel cold to the touch – this should not take longer than 5 minutes – drain and pack into containers or bags and place in the freezer immediately.

Should you require the frozen vegetables to be free-flow (loose, so that you can take just a limited quantity from the container or bag), place them when blanched on a baking tray or a special plastic tray until they are frozen, when they can be poured into a suitable bag or container.

Colour
Garlic cloves – stand back . . . you can almost smell them! Garlic is something you either love or can't abide, but for those with an eye on their health, some medics reckon that garlic is a good watchdog against the evils that cause heart attacks (Picture: Thompson & Morgan)

Herbes

Vegetable freezing guide

Vegetable	Preparation	Blanching	Packing	Freezer life	To use
Artichoke, Globe	Remove coarse outer leaves, trim stems and wash	7 mins	In rigid containers	12 months	Cook direct from freezer in boiling water
Artichoke, Jerusalem	Boil until soft, then liquidize to a purée	—	In rigid containers	3 months	Reheat purée straight from freezer
Asparagus	Remove woody ends, wash and scrape to remove scales	Thin stems—2 mins. Thcik stems—4 mins	In rigid containers	9 months	Cook direct from freezer in boiling water
Aubergine	Wash and cut into thick slices	4 mins	In plastic bags or rigid containers with greaseproof paper between layers	12 months	Cook direct from freezer in boiling water
Broad Beans	Shell	2 mins	In plastic bags	12 months	Cook direct from freezer in boiling water
Dwarf French Beans	Wash, trim ends and remove any strings	Whole—3 mins Sliced—2 mins	In plastic bags	12 months	Cook direct from freezer in boiling water
Runner Beans	Wash, trim ends and string. Cut into thick slices	2 mins	In plastic bags	12 months	Cook direct from freezer in boiling water
Beetroot	Wash, cook until tender. Rub off skins. Slice large beetroots	—	In rigid containers	6 months	Thaw overnight in fridge
Sprouting Broccoli	Trim outer leaves, wash and cut into stems of even lengths	Thin stems—3 mins. Thick stems—4 mins	In rigid containers	12 months	Cook direct from freezer in boiling water

Colour

Above left Lettuce 'Arctic King' – one of those lovely little varieties you sow in the autumn, allow to overwinter in the garden and then crop early in the spring. Taste is excellent (Picture: Garden News)

Below left Beetroot 'Bolthardy' – as the name suggests, this variety has an almost perfect resistance to running to seed from an early sowing. Rich maroon in colour, the taste is fresh and sweet (Picture: Thompson & Morgan)

Above right Courgette 'True French' – should be harvested when 3in (7.5cm) long and cooked unpeeled as they have tender skins. In fact, you fry them in butter in the same way as sausages (Picture: Thompson & Morgan)

Below right Chinese cabbage 'W.R' – acknowledged as a distinct improvement on most of the existing varieties, this can be cooked like an ordinary cabbage or eaten raw like lettuce (Picture: Ian and Stuart Unwin)

Vegetable	Preparation	Blanching	Packing	Freezer life	To use
Brussels Sprouts	Wash and grade into sizes	Small sprouts—3 mins. Medium—4 mins	In plastic bags	12 months	Cook direct from freezer in boiling water
Cabbage	Wash and shred	1½ mins	In plastic bags	9 months	Cook direct from freezer in boiling water
Carrots	Slice off tops, wash and scrape. Slice large carrots	Whole carrots—3 mins. Sliced—2 mins	In plastic bags	12 months	Cook direct from freezer in boiling water
Cauliflower	Strip leaves, wash and break into sprigs	3 mins	In plastic bags	6 months	Cook direct from freezer in boiling water
Celeriac	Wash, trim, scrape and cut into large slices	4 mins	In plastic bags	6 months	Cook direct from freezer in boiling water
Celery	Wash and cut into 2in (5cm) lengths	3 mins	In plastic bags	9 months	Do not use raw. Use as cooked vegetable or in soups and stews
Chicory	Remove bruised leaves and trim stalks	2 mins	In rigid containers	9 months	Cook direct from the freezer. Cannot be used in salads
Kale	Remove young, tender leaves from stem and wash	2 mins	In plastic bags	9 months	Cook direct from freezer in boiling water
Kohl Rabi	Cut off tops and scrub. Dice large specimens	Whole—3 mins Sliced—2 mins	In plastic bags	12 months	Cook direct from freezer in boiling water
Leeks	Remove outer leaves, cut off green tops and wash. Slice thick stems into rings	Whole—4 mins Sliced—2 mins	In plastic bags	6 months	Cook direct from freezer in boiling water
Lettuce	Wash. Separate into leaves or leave hearts whole	2 mins	In rigid containers	6 months	Thaw and braize, or add direct from freezer to soups
Marrows and Courgettes	Marrows—peel and slice Courgettes—wipe clean and cut into slices	Marrows—3 mins Courgettes—2 mins	In plastic bags	Marrows—10 months Courgettes—12 months	Thaw overnight in fridge
Onions	Peel and chop or slice large onions	2 mins	In plastic bags	6 months	Add to dishes while still frozen

Vegetable	Preparation	Blanching	Packing	Freezer life	To use
Parsnips	Scrub, trim and peel, cut into thin strips	2 mins	In plastic bags	9 months	Add direct from freezer, to stews and soups, or cook as required
Peas	Pod	1 min	In plastic bags	12 months	Cook direct from freezer in boiling water
Peppers	Wash, cut off stems and remove seeds and membrane. Leave whole or slice	Whole—3 mins Sliced—2 mins	In plastic bags	12 months	Thaw whole peppers for 3 hours. Add sliced peppers to dishes direct from freezer
Potatoes	Uncooked—wash and scrape. Chipped—fry for 2 mins in oil and drain	Uncooked—4 mins	In plastic bags	Uncooked—12 months. Chipped —6 months	Cook direct from freezer in boiling water. Chipped—deep fry direct from freezer
Pumpkin	Wash, peel and remove seeds and strings. Steam or boil until tender, then mash	—	In rigid containers	12 months	Cook direct from freezer in boiling water
Salsify	Trim and scrub	2 mins. Then peel while still warm	Cut into 3in (8cm) lengths—in plastic bags	12 months	Cook direct from freezer in boiling water
Spinach	Remove stems, wash and strip leaves off stalk	2 mins	In plastic bags	12 months	Cook direct from freezer in a little butter
Swede	Peel and cut into slices	3 mins	In plastic bags	12 months	Cook direct from freezer in boiling water
Sweet Corn	Strip off leaves and silk threads, cut off stems and grade for size	Small—4 mins Medium—6 mins Large—8 mins	Whole cobs in plastic bags	12 months	Thaw whole cobs overnight in fridge and cook in boiling water
Tomatoes	Whole or halved—wipe, remove stems and cut. Purée—wipe, chop, simmer in their own juice until soft and rub through a sieve. Juice—chop and sieve	2 seconds	Whole or halved in plastic bags. Juice and purée—in rigid containers	12 months	Whole and halved —add to soups stews or grill direct from freezer. Juice—thaw overnight in fridge and season. Purée—thaw overnight in fridge and use as required
Turnip	Trim and peel. Slice larger turnips	Whole—4 mins Sliced—2 mins	In plastic bags	12 months	Cook direct from freezer in boiling water

Fruit freezing guide

Fruit	Preparation	Blanching	Packing	Freezer life	To use
Apples	Uncooked—peel, core, cut into ½in (13mm) slices and drop in water to which lemon juice has been added to avoid discoloration. Purée—Cook slices until tender, rub through a sieve and cool	Uncooked—1 min	Uncooked—in plastic bags. Purée—in rigid containers	6 months	Thaw at room temperature and use as quickly as possible to prevent discoloration
Apricot	Wash, halve and remove stones.	½ min	In rigid containers	12 months	Thaw in fridge for 3 hours
Berries	Make sure fruit is dry	—	In plastic bags	12 months	Thaw in fridge for 6 hours
Cherries	Wash, dry and stone	—	In rigid containers	12 months	Thaw at room temperature for 3 hours
Currants—Red, White and Black	Wash and dry	—	In plastic bags	12 months	Thaw at room temperature for 3 hours
Figs	Wash and cut off stems	—	In rigid containers	12 months	Thaw at room temperature for 2 hours
Gooseberry	Top, tail and wash	—	In plastic bags	12 months	Thaw at room temperature for 1 hour
Grapes	Except for seedless (which can be frozen whole), skin, cut in half and remove pips. Prepare a syrup of 8oz (250gm) of sugar to 1pt (½l) of water	—	In rigid containers and cover with syrup	12 months	Thaw at room temperature for 3 hours
Peaches	Prepare a syrup as above but add abscorbic acid to it. Peel, halve and sugar to 1pt (½ litre) of water	—	In rigid containers	12 months	Thaw in fridge for 4 hours. Serve while still frosty

Fruit	Preparation	Blanching	Packing	Freezer life	To use
Pears	Peel, quarter and remove core. Add pieces to syrup (prepared as above). Poach for 1½ minutes, drain and cool	—	In rigid containers and cover with syrup	12 months	Thaw in fridge for 3–4 hours
Plums	Wipe, halve and stone	—	In rigid containers	12 months	Thaw overnight in fridge
Rhubarb	Wash, trim and slice	1 minute	In rigid containers	12 months	Cook straight from freezer
Strawberries	Choose only small, firm and dry berries. Do not wash	—	In rigid containers	12 months	Thaw at room temperature for 3 hours. Serve whole strawberries while still frosty

Blanching

1 Clean and divide into florets.

2 Place florets in blanching basket.

3 Plunge blanching basket into boiling water.

4 After blanching time, plunge into iced water.

5 Dry and place on tray.

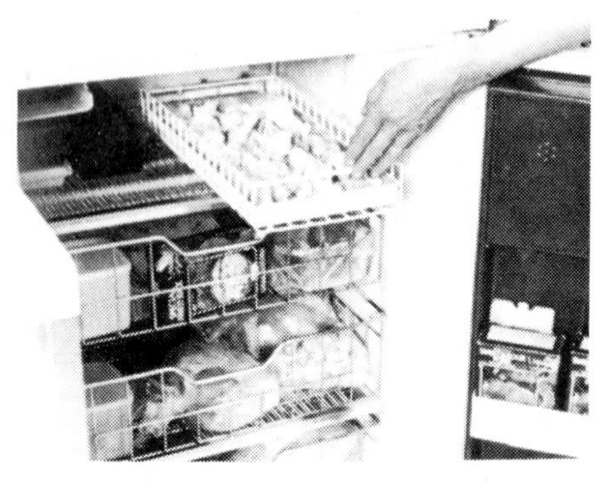

6 Insert tray in coldest part of freezer.

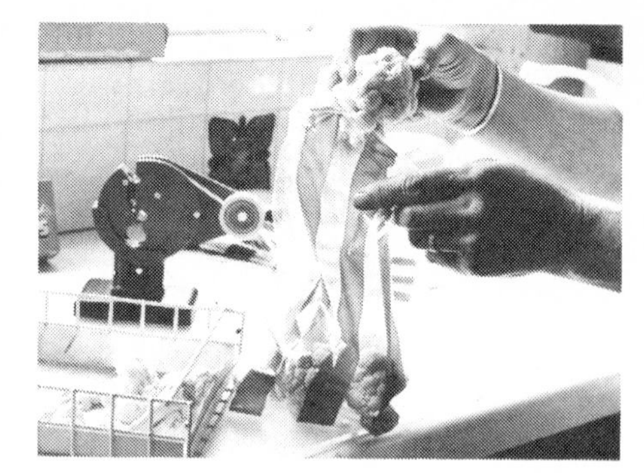

7 When frozen, place in plastic tray (or rigid container).

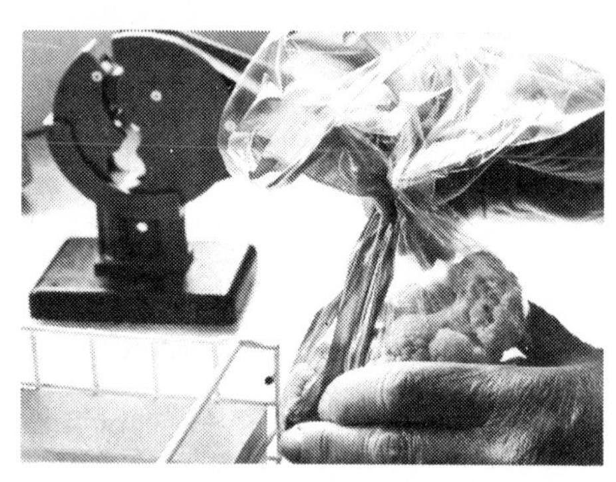

8 Extract air before sealing.

Preparing apples . . .

1 Prepare bowl of salted water.

2 Peel and core apples.

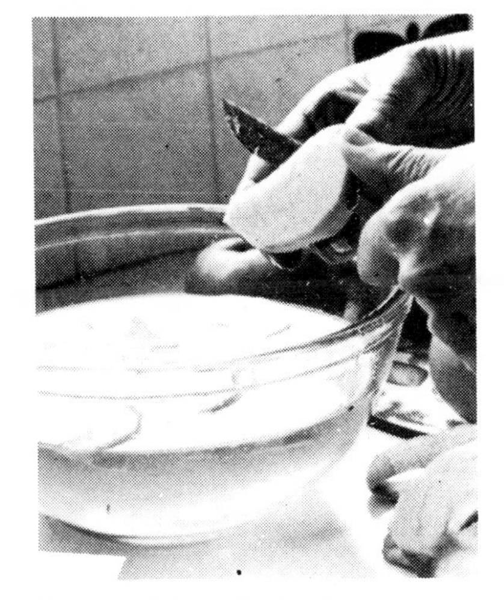

3 Slice into salted water.

4 Rinse under tap.

5 Blanch as for vegetables.

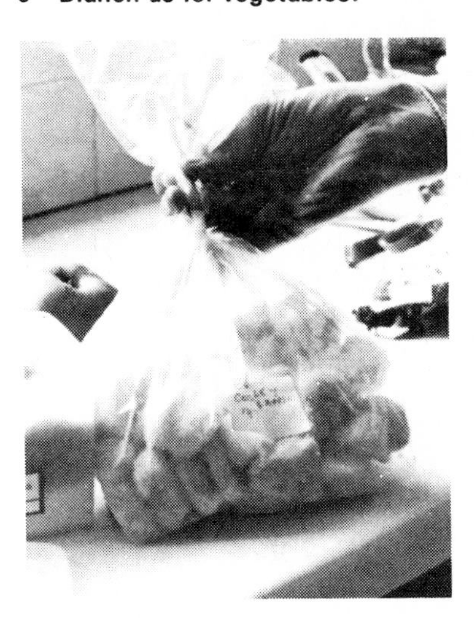

6 Pack in bags.

. . . and rhubarb

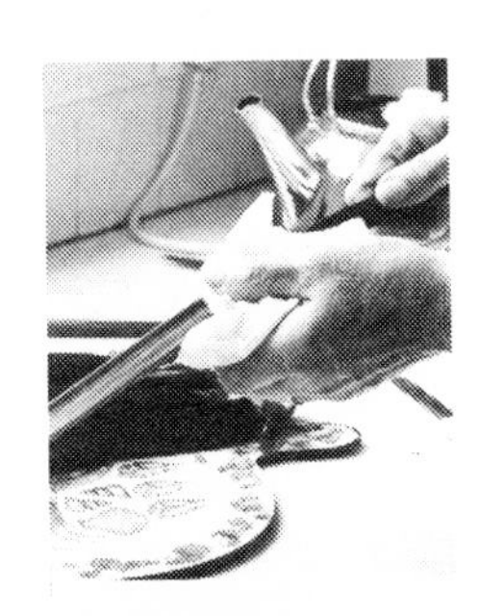

1 Wipe clean.

2 Slice into pieces.

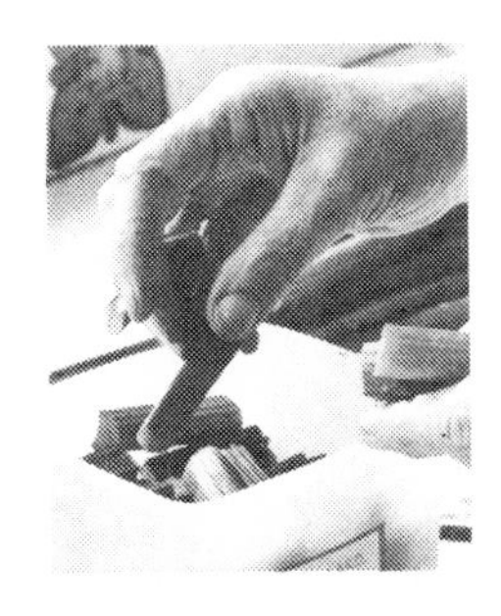

3 Pack in containers.

Storing and Pickling

It's possible these days to store almost all kinds of vegetables in a deep freeze. The surplus of the rich summer months can then be drawn on right through the long dark days of winter, and if properly done they lose none of their flavour or nutritional value.

For those without a freezer, peas and haricot beans can be dried, runner beans salted and tomatoes bottled, all with complete success. And many vegetables can be used for making chutneys and pickles.

There is no real need, however, to freeze, pickle or dry many of the root vegetables. Some can be left in the garden all through the winter to dig as wanted, others can be harvested and stored in different ways.

One cardinal rule must be followed. Any vegetable put into store must be sound. Damaged or diseased specimens will not only go rotten, but will rot others stored with them.

Store only the best. Sort them over at harvesting time and be prepared to look them over at intervals throughout the winter. Damaged specimens need not be thrown away but should be used immediately.

Vegetables that are best harvested and stored through winter

	Method	Period of Use
Haricot beans	Pick when ripe, shell dry and keep in jars	All year round
Beetroot	Pile, preferably against wall or fence, and cover with 6in (15cm) sand	November until April
Cabbage (**Winter keeping**)	Cut in November and keep on a shelf or in nets in cold outhouse	December, January, February
Carrot	As for beetroot	November to April
Celeriac	As for beetroot	November to April
Chicory	Dig roots in November, store in sand and force in the dark	All times from December to March
Onions	Ripen well in September/October; store in outhouse in nets	November to April
Potatoes	Dig and dry quickly, and store in sacks in a dark, frost-proof but cool place	November to May
Shallots	As for onions	November to March
Swedes and turnips in cold places	As for carrots and beetroot	November to February

Marrows can be cut when ripe and will keep for several weeks hung up in nets in frost-proof place. Green tomatoes will ripen progressively until Christmas if kept in drawers in warm rooms.

Vegetables that can be dug or picked as needed through winter

	Period of Use
Artichokes (**Jerusalem**)	September to February
Brussels sprouts	October to March
Cabbage (**savoys, late**) **and January King**	November to March
Celery	October to January
Leeks	November to April
Parsnips	September to April
Swedes and turnips in all but coldest places	October to March

If ground is needed for digging, parsnips and leeks can be dug up in February and set close together in another spot in the garden.

Chutneys and pickles

Green tomatoes that are fully grown at the end of the season will ripen quite naturally with keeping. But any that fail to reach full size may not be mature, and these, even if they do turn red, will lose their firmness and very often shrivel and become unattractive.

Ripen the big ones by all means, but don't waste the others, they make marvellous chutney. And made at the end of the tomato season, it's just right to go with the cold turkey on Boxing Day.

Those very useful vegetables, shallots, are, as a rule, grown specially for pickling. If they've done well in some years, the largest from the clumps will easily take the place of onions.

The next size down are the ones to select for seed, and the remainder, no matter how small, can go into the pickle jar.

Onions too, of course, make great pickles. No one tries to grow small onions, but among the seed rows there are almost bound to be some a lot smaller than others. And these, although many people think they are lacking a subtle something found in shallots, are a welcome mouth-watering addition to many a meal.

Chutneys

Chutney is a smooth thick mixture of cooked fruits, dried fruits, onions, spices, salt, sugar and vinegar.

Popular fruits to use are gooseberries, plums, rhubarb, and green tomatoes, and below are the recipes for the two most commonly-made chutneys – apple and ripe tomato.

Apple chutney
3lb (1.35kg) apples, 2pt (1.15l) vinegar, 1lb (455gm) onions, ¼lb (115gm) raisins, 1½lb (680gm) brown sugar, 1oz (28gm) ground ginger, 1oz (28gm) salt, ½ teaspoon cayenne pepper.

Wash, peel, core and cut up apples. Put pieces in large pan and cover with vinegar. Peel and chop onions, finely, and wash and chop raisins. Add both to apples.

Add rest of ingredients and put over heat. Heat slowly until sugar has dissolved, bring to boil, then simmer slowly until the chutney is thick and smooth, stirring occasionally. This will take 1–1½ hours.

When the chutney has a consistency similar to very thick cream, pour into jars, filling to within ½in (13mm) of the top. Fasten jars with screw lids or cellophane covers held in place by rubber bands.

Label jars and store in a cool, dry place, allowing the chutney to mature for a few months before using.

Tomato chutney
2lb (910gm) ripe tomatoes, 1lb (455gm) apples, ½lb (230gm) onions, ½lb (230gm) sultanas, 1lb (455gm) brown sugar, 1pt (570ml) vinegar, 1 teaspoon ground ginger, 1 teaspoon mixed spice, ½ teaspoon cayenne pepper, 1 tablespoon salt.

Prepare pan of boiling water and bowl of cold water. Dip tomatoes one at a time into boiling water for 5 seconds, then plunge them into cold water. Peel and cut up.

Peel, core and chop apples and peel and chop onions finely. Wash sultanas.

Put all ingredients in large pan. Cook slowly until sugar dissolves, then simmer gently for 1–1½ hours until thick and smooth.

Pickles

Pickled vegetables and fruit make appetising extras for almost any main dish or savoury snack. As with chutneys, almost any produce can be pickled, but the two most popular pickles are onions and piccalilli.

Pickled onions
4lb (1.8kg) onions, 2pt (1.15l) vinegar, ½lb (230gm) salt, 1 small stick cinnamon, 6 cloves, 5 pieces mace, 3 bay leaves, 1 dessertspoon whole-spice.

Cut off ends of onions, peel and pack in layers in mixing bowl with the salt. Cover and leave to stand for 24 hours.

Tie the spices (cinnamon, cloves, mace, bay leaves and wholespice) in small piece of muslin and put spice bag and vinegar in a pan and bring to the boil. Remove from heat and pour into a jug or basin. Remove spices when vinegar is quite cold and store vinegar in sealed bottles.

After 24 hours, pack onions tightly into jars, but leave neck of the jars free. Cover with the spiced vinegar. The level of the vinegar should be ½in (13mm) above the onions.

Fasten jars with screw lids, label and store.

Piccalilli

This is a mixture of fresh, crisp vegetables in a mustard sauce.

1lb (455gm) small onions, 1lb (455gm) marrow, 1 small cauliflower, ½ cucumber, ½lb (230gm) runner beans, 4pt (2.3l) water, ½lb (230gm) salt, 3oz (85gm) flour, 2oz (60gm) mustard, ½oz (15gm) turmeric powder, 2pt (1.15l) vinegar.

Peel and cut vegetables up into chunks. Put the salt in a large mixing bowl, add the water, stir until dissolved, then add the vegetables. Cover and leave for 24 hours.

Next day, drain the vegetables in a colander.

Blend flour, mustard and turmeric with a little of the vinegar in a large pan. Add rest of vinegar and stir over gentle heat until it thickens and boils. Add the vegetables and cook slowly for 3–4 minutes until warmed through. The vegetables must not soften.

Pack the vegetables into heated jars, then pour in sufficient mustard sauce to cover them. Fasten jars with screw lids, label and store for a few weeks before use.

Glossary

Acid soil
Low in, or without lime
Alkaline soil
With lime
Annual
A plant that lives and dies all in one season

Balanced fertiliser
One containing all the important plant foods
Biennial
A plant that lives over two seasons and then dies
Blanching
Excluding light from stems as in celery
Blanching (for freezing)
Scalding produce in boiling water for a specific period of time
Bleed
Lose sap/colour through a wound
Bolt
Make a seed stem
Brassicas
In general terms, members of the cabbage family
Broadcast
Sow seeds in patches rather than rows

Catch crop
A crop grown on ground that is waiting to grow a later crop
Check
A temporary halt in growth
Chit
Start to spurt
Clamp
A store for root vegetables – potatoes, carrots, beetroot, etc. – made outside by covering harvested crops with straw and soil
Compatible
Suitable for growing together
Compost
Partly rotted down garden waste
Cordons
Plants kept to a single growing stem
Crown
The part of a plant where stems and roots meet
Cultivar
Variety
Cuttings
Small lengths of a plant put in to make roots

Deciduous
Loses leaves in winter
Double digging
Turning over the top spadeful of soil and breaking up lower ground with a fork
Drill
A small trench into which seeds are sown

Earthing up
To draw soil up to the stems of plants
Espalier
Trees trained flat with upright trunk and horizontal branches
Evergreen
Able to hold its leaves through the winter

F1 hybrids
First generation plants from two carefully controlled parents
Force
To make grow out of season
Frost pocket
Area where frost is likely

Germinate
The action of seed coming to life
Glut
Too many at a time
'Greens'
The cabbage family
Growing bags
Polythene bags of no-soil compost in which plants can be grown

Hardened off
Gradually got used to cooler conditions
Hardy
Able to resist frost
Haulms
Top growth of plants, particularly potatoes, peas, beans, etc.
Heeled in
Temporary planting in a sloping position
Humus
Decomposing animal and/or vegetable matter
Inter-cropping
Growing one crop between the rows of another

John Innes
A mixture of soil, peat, sand and fertiliser

Levington
A proprietary no-soil compost
Lifted
Dug up

Mulch
A covering of manure or similar over the root area of plants

Nursery bed
A piece of ground where small plants are set to grow on before moving to their permanent positions

Offsets
A small growth from the bottom of a plant capable of being taken off to make a new plant
Organic
Consisting of vegetable or animal matter

Pelleted seed
Seeds enclosed in a small capsule for easy sowing
Perennial
A plant that produces growth year after year
Pollinator
A variety whose pollen will help to 'set' other varieties
Pot bound
In a pot too long, resulting in overcrowded roots
Potted on
Moved from a smaller pot into a larger pot
Pricked out
Transplanted a little further apart, generally into boxes

Root drill
The ball of compost or soil and roots carried by plants from a pot
Rootstock
The root part of a grafted plant; also the crown of a herbaceous plant
Rotation
Moving different families of crops around the garden from year to year
Runners
Small plants produced on growths coming from old plants

Seed leaves
The first two leaves the plant makes
Self blanching
Needing no covering to assist blanching
Self fertile
A plant able to set fruit with its own pollen
'Set'
Fruit has started to form
Sideshoots
Growths which arise generally from leaf joints on a main stem
Soft
Unable to stand hard weather
Spit
A spade's depth of soil
Standard trees
With a clear stem of 6ft (1.8m)
Suckers
A shoot arising from an underground stem
Systemic
Works from the inside of the plant

Thinning out
Removing surplus plants or shoots
Tilth
A fine top layer of soil necessary for seed sowing
Top dressing
Fertiliser applied to the surface of the soil
Transplant
Move a plant from one place to another
Truss
Bunch of flowers or fruit
Tuber
A swollen underground root that serves as a food store

Water in
Apply water from a can to individual plants at setting out time

Index